LOST IN SIBERIA

To
Susanne
Best wishes. Enjoy!
Vivian Lukes
FRANK WARD

LOST IN
SIBERIA
my education in the
former Soviet Union

VIVIAN LESKES

photographs by FRANK WARD

Haley's
Athol, Massachusetts

Haley's
488 South Main Street
Athol, Massachusetts 01331
haley.antique@verizon.net
1.800.215.8805

front cover photo:
The author on the bank of the Angara River, Irkutsk, Siberia, 2008
by Frank Ward

International Standard Book Number: 978-1-884540-89-9
Library of Congress Catalog Number: 2010940761

For Tobey and Caleb

Contents

Photographs

All photographs are ©2011 by Frank Ward.

Author's Note

The use of italics indicates a conversation conducted in Russian or words in Russian or a language not English. Conversations not italicized were conducted in English.

The selection of photographs is intended to capture the mood of the essay rather than to illustrate it.

Exploring Language and Finding Fresh Worlds

an introduction by Vivian Leskes

Although these essays were written between 2001 and 2008 during three trips to the former Soviet Union, the seed of this story was planted long ago, maybe even before I was born.

My Grandma Lottie had always warned me that my grandfather was not a good man. An elementary school principal, he retired young and abandoned his wife and three children to travel the world with nothing but a backpack and the attractive kindergarten teacher from his school. When he was in New York, Grandpa Frank lived in a residential hotel with books piled high on every surface. He studied nine languages, only reading literature in the original. He didn't stop traveling until he became mortally ill in Argentina at the age of seventy, at which time his mistress brought him home to die. I was ten at that time. Although Grandma Lottie disapproved, my mother gave me a photo of her father on the streets of New York, trim and upright, curly gray hair and mustache, his backpack on his back.

A few months later, an old man in a fedora, with hunched shoulders, rang our doorbell in the Bronx. In a heavy Eastern European accent, he explained that he was recruiting children in the community to study Yiddish. My parents were assimilated Jews; they considered themselves leftists and atheists. I had never attended temple. I knew nothing about Judaism; I didn't even know that only Jews spoke Yiddish. All I knew was that it was a foreign language, and, to my mother's consternation, I immediately said that I wanted to join the Yiddish class; I wanted to learn to speak another language like Grandpa and explore the world.

We sat in a musty basement classroom in an old apartment building. Pipes snaked around the low ceiling; paint was chipping

1

off the walls. His fedora still on his head, Mr. Gimpelstein walked between aisles of seats, droning Yiddish sentences to the beat of a wooden ruler as we repeated. *"Berele iz a yingele. In der fri Berele shteyt uf. Berele geyt in shul."* When the teacher wasn't looking, we passed notes and poked each other. Mr. Gimpelstein yelled and wagged his ruler. After a month, I told my mother I'd had enough of learning Yiddish. It was a brief moment in my life, a few steps along a path that led nowhere, but it was a harbinger of a lifelong fascination with languages and a lesson in how not to teach them.

I left that enclave in the Bronx, lived and worked in rural Mexico and southern France. I learned to speak Spanish and French. I met my photographer husband, also a Frank, in Geneva when he was returning from a year in India and Nepal. After our wedding, we traveled for another year with backpacks, like my grandfather, overland from Europe to Asia, ahead of a revolution in Iran and a war in Afghanistan. Then we settled down to raise a family in my husband's native Massachusetts, and I taught English as a Second Language at a community college. While the children were young, my Frank continued to travel and photograph in countries where the children and I couldn't follow him, in Bosnia and Kosovo after the wars there, in Tibet when it was first opened by the Chinese. He won a grant to go to India; I stayed home with our daughter and son, stoking the wood stove, driving the children to sports and music lessons, making pickles and jams from the garden.

During those years, the faces of my students, Puerto Rican, Uzbek, Russian, Korean, Tibetan, Colombian, Congolese, too many to count, were the faces of the world for me. Looking out at them, helping them in their struggles with a new language and a new culture, I could almost forget that I was living in a small New England town. I advised my students in Spanish. I studied French grammar. It was almost like being abroad—almost—but the first time I crossed an international border after five years—and that border was merely from Vermont to Québec—I cried with joy.

That childish impulse to join the Yiddish class so many years ago reminds me now of my decision in 2001 to use my sabbatical to participate in an exchange program between my community college and a university in Ukraine. My role there was to mentor English language faculty and model American teaching methodology. I didn't know where I was going; I had no concept of Ukraine or Ukrainian culture. I didn't know that my grandfather had been born in Kiev. I didn't know that I would find in the Ukrainian markets the ethnic foods of my childhood, the half-sour pickles, the blintzes, the halvah, the sesame seed candies, the smoked fish. I joined the exchange project on an ignorant whim; perhaps, to be honest, it was merely my turn to go as far as I could go.

I had no idea that the trip would spark my imagination for years. My grandfather's neglect of his family was no model for me, but since that first excursion into the former Soviet Union, I have taken or created every opportunity to return there. I had no premonition that Ukraine would lead me to Russia and Russia to Central Asia, that it would be a journey deep as well as far, to the foreign and the strangely familiar, from the Gulf of Finland to the Sea of Japan, that I would be sheltered in the warm embrace of unconditional friendship and abandoned in the Siberian deep freeze. This adventure, and I suspect it isn't finished yet, has exposed me to a world that I both revere and mock, introduced me to the contradictions of a vast empire, and seduced me with those very paradoxes. The journey has been by plane and train and the maddening *marshrutki*, the minivan transport that all Russians love to hate. But it has also been the journey of a language teacher roaming in the English classrooms of the former Soviet Union, where the rules of grammar are clearer than the logic of the society. It has been a journey, as well, of a language student wandering in the depths of the unconquerable, achingly majestic language of Russian. These essays are a product of this ongoing exploration.

When I returned to the community college in September 2008, after my Fulbright semester in Irkutsk, Siberia, I saw Rudolfo, an ESL student from a Siberian city an overnight train ride from my post in Irkutsk.

"How was your trip?" he asked.

"I miss Siberia," I said, knowing I was insane to feel that way.

"Did you find the winter cold?"

"It was -30°C (-22°F) when we arrived," I said.

"Beautiful," he said, his eyes shining. "I love that."

And I knew just how he felt.

Church, Irkutsk, Siberia. 2008

I Arrive in Poltava

Outside my window, a man in a gray coat and cap bicycles down the muddy road past little brick houses, each with a peaked tin roof. The Ukrainian crows pick at the trash strewn along the road. The sky is gray; the roads are wet, but it isn't raining. The town seems calm. A woman in boots and a scarf tied under her chin returns from the market, a shopping bag under each arm.

I have arrived in the provinces. First was the overnight trans-Atlantic flight to Frankfurt, then an exhausting four-hour wait at the airport. On the shorter flight to Kiev, the passengers were nearly all male, big pale serious-looking men loaded with parcels filled, I imagined, with goods from the West. I could feel we were heading into the hinterland.

The young couple next to me ate the airplane breakfast with great gusto, every piece of cheese, both roll and croissant, all the butter, all the jam, the eggs and meat, the yogurt. They drank orange juice, and tomato juice, and coffee. ("They were surely Ukrainian," Svetlana, the Ukrainian English teacher, said later. "We always eat everything and ask for more.")

In Kiev the porters found us, the American teachers, right away. One descended on Joanne, my colleague, in her pale blue warm-up suit, and then another spotted me. They gave us brusque instructions for filling out our declaration forms and then, without a smile, informed us that the charge for their services was twenty dollars. But, in the company of these large stern men, the customs officer let me pass without opening my suitcase. This was just as well since it contained two dozen packs of illicit garden seeds and garlic from

9

my garden, four boxes of Ziploc bags, six pairs of knee-high panty hose, two hundred individually wrapped pieces of red licorice, thirty pens, children's vitamins, Beanie Babies, and a figure-skating Barbie, all gifts for our many hosts.

Two beggars followed us as the porters dragged our bags to the waiting university van. "The Americans have arrived," they all must have said to themselves.

"Don't ever speak English in front of a taxi driver," Svetlana said. "You will pay ten times over for the fare."

The trip from the airport was long and foggy past muddy fallow fields with not a town in sight for five hours. From what I could see through steamed windows, the land was flat, fields bordered by leafless trees. Occasionally we passed a birch forest. Small squat women walked down the highway dragging entire trees for firewood. Along the wet road, an occasional vendor huddled at a table, selling potatoes or meat or smoked fish. At the entrance to Poltava region, we stopped, and Svetlana pulled a picnic from her basket, thick slabs of roast pork and cheese, fresh dark bread, homemade pickles, a thermos of hot tea, cookies, and chocolate. We ate in the car, the cold damp air outside uninviting. The driver said nothing, ate nothing, smoked his cigarettes, and drove on. By the end of the trip we traveled in thick and total fog. The road was invisible; cars loomed suddenly from nowhere. The driver magically turned off the highway onto unseen roads. In my groggy exhaustion, it seemed that I was being transported to a very remote place.

Through the night fog, the city of Poltava emerged, bright and cosmopolitan compared to the long, lonely expanses. There was a glimpse of wide tree-lined streets, shops, people in long coats on the boulevards. We were whisked into the university residence, hugged in welcome by the concierge. Young blond male students carried our suitcases one flight up to our apartments, and we had arrived.

University students, Siberia. 2008

I Begin Teaching

Teaching at Poltava University is like teaching on the other side of Alice's Looking Glass, different from any academic institution I have ever experienced. I can't understand how it manages to produce an educated student body.

Each day students arrive at school with no idea where their classes will meet. A sheet is posted daily on a bulletin board in the main lobby announcing room assignments. The faculty doesn't know where or when the classes will meet either. In three places on my schedule it is written that I teach Natalya Sergeiovna's English class at 10 AM on Thursdays. The odd thing is that Natalya and I both arrived at the classroom at 11:40, not 10. The students also came at 11:40. How did we all know to meet at that time?

There are many remnants of the Soviet mentality: don't give anyone too much information; keep people waiting and anxious. In the office I share with other English teachers, a row of chairs lines one wall. One of Olga's students Zhenyia comes into the office. He would like to borrow a copy of *Entertainment* magazine; it's a year old, but it arrived yesterday in a box from the States.

Olga and I are in the middle of a discussion on the merits of salt pickles as opposed to vinegar pickles. "Take a seat please," Olga says to Zhenyia with a wave toward the empty chairs. She turns back to me. "I always put a piece of horseradish in each pickle jar. It's a requirement."

Another student Sveta enters, and then Fyodor. Each patiently takes a seat next to Zhenyia until there is a Soviet style queue waiting to borrow the out-of-date magazines. By now I

15

have heard Olga's opinion of preserving sauerkraut, and we have moved on to making jams and compote. The message to the students, who all understand our conversation in English, is that Olga and I are too important to be bothered with their needs.

Apparently, this occurs at all levels of society. My American colleague Joanne and I have an appointment to meet Nikolai Aleksandrvitch, rector of the university. Yesterday, when we tried to arrange a time for today, we were told the time hadn't been determined yet. This morning at 8 AM at home, we get a call that the rector will see us at 10. We arrive on time, but his door is closed. His secretary waves us toward the row of chairs.

Someone in the infinite layers of bureaucracy is reveling in his exalted state while I wait nervously. My passport was whisked off for some obligatory inspection a few days after we arrived. Every day I ask for my passport and am put in the queue. Maybe someone is expecting a little silver across the palm to move the process along more swiftly.

Communication at the university is by face-to-face contact only. No internal e-mail, no answering machines or voice mail, no inter-office telephones, no printed information at all. In order to inform the dining room that I will not be at lunch today, it is necessary to go down four flights of stairs, walk over to the next building, and speak directly with the ladies in the dining hall. The fact that they must be told in Russian or Ukrainian is just one communication barrier among many.

Paper is a precious commodity, so nothing is printed and handed out. An overhead projector is an impossibility. Even a blackboard seems to be too much to expect. When it does exist in a classroom, it is about four feet square. The chalk is an irregular chunk that looks as if it has been chopped directly from a quarry.

The eraser is a rag that a student will occasionally moisten from a rest room. Teachers do not seem to use blackboards. They sit in front of the class and work directly from a text without deviating.

"Do you have your students work in pairs?" I ask Tatiana Ivanovna.

"Certainly, if the text says to do so."

I must be an oddity to students and teachers alike. I walk down the aisle or weave between desks to indicate linear or non-linear thinking. I explain the shape of an essay by drawing pictures. To show organized paragraphs, I draw neat geometric patterns and make squiggles to show disorganized paragraphs. I create ad hoc student groups and ask them to design model paragraphs and essays jointly. The students are responsive and somewhat amazed.

"We will hold our next class in this office," Olga says. "We will have everything we need. The only thing missing will be a blackboard."

"Blackboards are very helpful for language instruction," I say. "The student gets to see the information as well as hear it."

I meet five classes, each for one period a week, not enough to have a sense of continuity for any one group. The students all recognize me and say hello in the halls, but I don't know their names or which group they are in or which anecdotes I have told which classes.

This week I plan parallel lessons for four classes. One group hasn't received copies of the reading. Two classes give me writing samples; two do not. In one group, the teacher and students request an oral class rather than a writing class. In one class, the students ask for another hour with me a week. Classes do not seem to have a prescribed number of hours. Then another group hears that it is possible to get more time, so they request another hour too.

The fifth class is Olga's. She wants a literature-based class, using a different book, one that I warn her may be too difficult. Today before class, she asks me vocabulary and grammar questions.

I just need to remember the purpose of my presence. I am here to model instruction for the teachers, particularly writing instruction. So it is just as well that I have contact with many teachers and many students. I am not here to improve the skills of Pavel or Luda or any specific group of students. I am here to improve the teachers' skills.

In the midst of all this confusion, the students are bright and eager; Ukraine's new generation will have to make changes the older people will never make. The shy ones are gradually beginning to talk. Even Serge, who says "cool" all the time, is drawn into my explanation of how Russian speakers tend to write in English. He gives me his sample paragraph as soon as I enter the room and then watches for my reaction. The title is "Hookers of Poltava."

"Let's talk about sex in English," he says. This is not the first time I have heard this in a class. Some things don't change from one culture to the next.

"No," I say. "I'm not interested in talking with you about sex. Talk with your friends about that. It's not appropriate in class."

The other students nod their heads seriously. Serge, too, is nodding his head. I guess the American teacher gave the correct answer.

War memorial guard, Irkutsk, Siberia. 2008

Russian Language Student

Lyubov Ivanovna comes to my apartment three times a week to give me Russian lessons. In the days of the Soviet Union, she taught Russian as a Second Language at the university. At that time, there were many foreigners who came to study the economics of Soviet cooperatives. Since the rise of Ukrainian nationalism and the decision that all classes be conducted in Ukrainian, fewer foreign students now come to Ukraine. Lyubov has only five foreign students at the university now, two Iranians and three Jordanians. Even though instruction is now in Ukrainian, they still need to learn Russian since there are no textbooks in Ukrainian.

Lyubov supplements her much depleted income by providing me with private Russian lessons. I pay her five dollars per hour. Ukrainians are not supposed to do business in dollars, but they are all eager to do so since a hard currency provides protection against any sudden convulsions of the *greven*.

I am on page fifty-two in an ancient Soviet textbook. "*Eta kniga. Eta maya kniga. Eta maya staraya kniga.*"

I suspect the text is full of Soviet propaganda about how happy the students are to spend the summers working on the railroad, but at the moment, I'm just pleased I can read that Ivan and Irina are engineers who work in the institute.

So far, my progress in Russian has faced three barriers. Each would be serious alone, and together they are probably insurmountable. First, I am still struggling with the Cyrillic alphabet. Fifty years of pronouncing the letter *H* as in *house* keeps getting in my way of learning to pronounce it as in *nose*. B as in *visit*, P as in *rose*, Y as in *oodles*, X as in *Chanukah*. I am just getting used to the print version of Cyrillic when Lyubov insists that I write in cursive instead of printing.

"My grandmother writes like that," she says, pointing at my block letters.

If a Ukrainian grandmother is satisfied to print, that's good enough for me, but Lyubov doesn't see it that way. So now there is a second alphabet to learn. The cursive version of *t* looks like an *m*, the *p* looks like an *n*, the *d* looks like a *g*.

The second hindrance to learning Russian is its pronunciation.

"I think Russian should borrow some vowels from French," I tell my English class when they ask about my Russian.

One letter is pronounced like the combination of the final sound in *fresh* and the initial sound in *chicken*, shch. Just saying hello is impossible: *zdravstvuytye*.

The third hindrance is the grammar. I am a lover of grammar and a teacher of grammar, but this is an entirely new challenge for me. It must be indicative of a completely different world view I don't yet understand. Besides conjugating verbs, which I am used to from Spanish and French, and besides male, female, neuter, and plural nouns, Russian has six different endings for adjectives and nouns depending on how the noun is used in the sentence. The endings also vary with specific prepositions, and I don't know what else. Even proper names change. Sveta goes to Washington, but she is in *Washingtonye*. Studying Russian is one of the hardest things I have ever tried to do. I'll add it to figure skating, raising children, and meditating.

Lyubov seems pleased by my progress. She says that because I know Spanish and French, I'm learning fast, but to me the process is excruciating. Just the act of writing is so exhausting I often fall asleep over my Russian homework. After a two-hour lesson, I collapse on the bed.

We don't have a Russian-English dictionary, but Lyubov has found a Russian-Spanish commentary on the Soviet textbook. This new booklet includes the Russian vocabulary translated into Spanish. When I am struggling with a difficult concept, Lyubov says, "*Patom*." I don't understand *patom*, so she points to the Cyrillic block letters in my commentary, and I see *patom* means *luego* in Spanish, "later." So in my notebook, I write *patom* in cursive: but it looks like *nomow*. No problem. I'll learn this *nomow* .

Beach lady, Odessa, Ukraine. 2005

A Special Week

When my American colleague Joanne and I arrive at the university on Monday morning, Olga informs us we are invited to a special luncheon in the dining room at 1 PM. According to my schedule, I have two classes in a row from 11:40 to 2:30, so I can't make it to the luncheon.

"This is a special occasion," Olga says.

"I'm very sorry that I will have to miss it."

Tatiana Petrovna is the teacher of my first group. After the class she says, "So now you will go to lunch."

"No," I say." I have Mariya Ivanovna's class." At the request of Mariya's students, I have committed myself to an extra period of instruction. That group is very enthusiastic. They always greet me with broad smiles. They listen carefully and thank me after class.

"But it is a special lunch," Tatiana says. "You must not miss it." She goes in search of Mariya.

In a few minutes, Mariya meets me in the hall. "The students and I will wait for you," she says. "You must go to the luncheon; it's a special event."

When I arrive in the dining room, Joanne and Olga are seated with four women and one man, all faculty members. The first course is already before them, cabbage salad, the same as every other day. They are toasting Elena good luck for the defense of her dissertation. I clink my glass with the rest and take a sip of the cognac.

The lone man at the table motions to me to drink up.

"*I am a professor,*" I say in Russian. "*I have a class at 1:10.*"

He fills my glass to the brim and toasts to all professors. The conversation turns to professorial rank and degrees.

"There's an old Ukrainian expression," he says as Olga translates. *"If your work gets in the way of the cognac, it's time to abandon your work."*

I try to cover my glass when he pours for the third round.

The second course is Ukrainian borscht. It looks like soup, but they say it is borscht, not soup; they serve it to Joanne and me every day for lunch. I am trying to eat quickly, so I can get to my class.

"When there is silence at the table," the self-proclaimed toaster declares, *"it is time for more cognac."* He fills everyone's glass again and demands that Joanne make a toast. She obliges by lifting her glass to our academic accomplishments, past, present, and future.

The third course is the usual potatoes and meat, some kind of cylindrical pork something.

"This toast is bottoms up," the man declares.

I drain the glass and race out before the waitress can bring tea and dessert.

The students in Mariya's class stand when I arrive fifty minutes late. No one acts surprised or impatient, but they don't have the usual enthusiastic smiles. They just look worn down.

I am the only one who seems to feel an apology is in order. "In America," I say, "teachers cannot go to lunch when they are supposed to go to class. They cannot drink cognac before class." I make a slicing motion across my neck to indicate that the ax would fall.

The absurdity of American customs gets a laugh from the students.

On Tuesday, Olga tells us there is another special luncheon at 1 PM to celebrate the same occasion with the same people. Again,

I am supposed to meet Mariya's students. It is their regularly scheduled class time.

"I can't go," I say.

"Just have lunch and then go to class. The students will wait," Olga says.

"I can't do it to the same students twice."

"It's a special occasion."

"Absolutely not."

On Wednesday, there is a third special luncheon to celebrate Elena's impending doctoral examination.

"Please come today," Olga says.

"I hope Elena takes her oral examination soon," I say.

"We don't consider it good luck to mention the date."

"I am scheduled to meet your class, Olga."

"I have told the students to meet us here in the office. They will wait until we have lunch. This is a special week."

The first week I arrived was a special week. It was their practicum time; the students had to write business letters the whole time. The second week was so special that there were no English classes at all. I guess last week was not a special week, so that made it uniquely unremarkable. Now this is another special week.

I insist that I meet Olga's class although she doesn't seem to feel the same obligation. I ask her to change the room to one with a blackboard.

A dozen students meet me in an enormous lecture hall. There is a large blackboard, but Zhenyia must go out searching for a chunk of chalk. I bring the students down to the first couple of rows, and we discuss the assigned short story, "Thank You Ma'am" by Langston Hughes. We examine the setting, the African American speech, the actions of the characters. Then, on the

31

blackboard, I diagram how to write a descriptive essay in English, how to write an introduction, body, and conclusion. I show them how to make topic sentences for paragraphs and how to give supporting details. As a class, on the board, we create the skeleton of a sample essay that describes the character of the young boy in the story. I am leaving for the States for a month, so I assign the class their first essay to be ready when I return, a description of the character Mrs. Jones.

When the class is over, a student Sasha thanks me. "This is very important," he says. "Nobody has ever taught us this."

"The teachers haven't learned about organizing writing in English," I say. "That's why I am here, to show them how to teach writing."

Too bad Olga is at the special luncheon. But then, this is a special week.

Embrace, Moscow fountain. 2008

Singular and Plural

I returned to Poltava, Ukraine after four years.

In Russian, numbers one through four all seem to be singular since they are followed by singular nouns. Only with the number five do plural nouns appear. But the number one isn't singular precisely the way the number three is; one requires a singular noun of a different case. The literal translation would be *one person, two of a person, three of a person, four of a person, five of people. One car, two of a car, three of a car, four of a car, five of cars,* and so on. It seems that two, three, and four are in a special category, not quite singular and not quite plural. In old Russian, there was also a separate category for two of anything, a unique concept, with its own noun and adjectival endings in all six cases, distinct from singular, and also not plural.

I suppose the closest we come to the old Russian concept of two in English would be a pair or a couple: a pair of scissors or a pair of gloves or a couple of dollars. Noah's ark notwithstanding, in the English-speaking world, some things don't seem to go together even when there are two of them. We don't think of a couple of wars or a pair of telephone bills. Is our English language distinction between one and other-than-one a reflection of our need for individuality? Is it more essential for us English speakers to separate ourselves from others than it is for Russian speakers?

Varvara, who sells dried fruit in the market, is very happy that I can speak in Russian with her now, four years later, *woman to woman,* as she says. When I was here in 2001, her older son, Misha had to translate for us. At the time, that didn't stop Varvara from drinking large quantities of cognac and then discussing how lonely she had been since her divorce and, as Misha delicately put it, how a woman had "certain needs." At that time, she and her two sons, who were then eighteen and fourteen, lived in one room. Now they are all proud to show me the half-house they have purchased. Before the war the house belonged to a Ukrainian Jewish lawyer, and we all know what happened to him once the war began.

The house is a traditional one-story stucco-covered building with a peaked roof and wooden shutters. To get to it, we enter a yard off the street. Past the neighbor's half with the flourishing peony beds and vegetable garden is Varvara's half of the house, with a small covered porch and an unkempt garden plot.

Varvara explains that they have done a lot of renovation work. Misha tiled the bathroom himself; they have painted and wallpapered, and they all have big plans for the garden. The house has a lot of space by Ukrainian standards. There is a large kitchen with a root cellar for keeping pickles and potatoes. Through the kitchen is the living room where Varvara sleeps, and through the living room is a bedroom for the two sons. The bedroom also serves as the repository of the prized possessions of the family, the tea set and wineglasses stored in a glass-front cabinet, icons, photographs, a computer, and a lovely antique table they found in the house when they moved in. I suppose the Jewish lawyer left in a hurry.

Private bedrooms are out of the question. I have never seen a house or apartment in Ukraine where there is such a thing as personal space. Usually the dining room table and a bed are in the same front room. Often the couch provides seats for two or three at the table and doubles as a bed at night. I think every Ukrainian couch is designed to open out into a bed.

During the four years that I have been away, Varvara had a lover, a man younger than she. He has since disappeared, but fortunately, not before he did a lot of the reconstruction on the house. I imagine he and Varvara slept in the walk-through living room, and her sons walked past them from their inner room to get to the kitchen or bathroom.

In this family, there is no youthful angst. The boys don't demand privacy or an allowance or independence from the family. If they earn any money, it goes into the common pot. I can't see Vanya or Misha slamming the bedroom door in a fit and shouting, "Leave me alone!"

Tonight, Misha, as the man of the house, cooks the *shashlik* over the open fire. His girlfriend Nastiya is present for our dinner together, and they steal a few kisses in the yard as he tends the sizzling skewers of marinated meat. It is common to see young people entwined on a park bench in the Center or smooching on the walking boulevard October Street. Their crowded apartments do not provide any privacy, so they prefer the anonymity of the street.

I am thankful that I don't need the translation help of Vanya or Misha when Varvara takes out the love letters she received by e-mail from some fellow in Hyannis, Mass. A computer program translated his letters from English into Russian. "*Varvara, I am looking for someone to share my life. You are a beautiful sexy woman. When I look at your photograph, I long to hold you in my arms and kiss you all over.*" I wonder what her sons think of the photos of their mother on the Internet, the forty-five-year-old woman, burnt orange hair piled high on her head, the black dress too low cut and too short. Surely they are aware of the photographs, since nothing seems to be secret or private in this country, and Varvara probably needed her sons' help to upload them.

"This man is a professional," she says. *"He has a business. He said money is not a problem. He said he would come here to meet me during his vacation."* She shows me his picture, a heavyset balding man in front of the ocean.

"Varvara, this may not be true. You don't know who he really is."

She looks sorrowful. *"He hasn't written for a while. A man who is my age wants a woman who is twenty-five."*

At midnight, when it is time for me to leave, Vanya says, "Tomorrow I will have my graduation celebration. Would you like to come? I will dance the waltz."

I can't imagine an American high school student inviting a gray-haired stranger to watch him dance. "I would be honored to attend."

Waiting in the street is a taxi. Misha and Nastiya snuggle in the back seat as they accompany me to my apartment. When I get out of the cab, they may have ten minutes to themselves, with the taxi driver, of course, three of a person in the cab together.

On the dock, Odessa, Ukraine. 2005

Simple Pleasures

On my way back from the market, there is a lady sitting on a stool on the sidewalk, at her feet an open sack of roasted peanuts. On top of the sack is a large cup measure filled to the top with peanuts; this she sells for two *grevna*, forty cents. A smaller cup costs one *greven*. I taste a peanut; it's well roasted and fresh, so I ask for a large cup.

"*Where are you from?*" she asks.

"*From America.*"

"*And what do you think of our place here?*"

My tote bag contains a kilo of homegrown cherries that I have just bought for sixty cents. During the last two hours at the market, I have made plans with Varvara to cook American chili at her home next week. I met an Uzbek man who sold me little bags of cumin and oregano for the chili and showed me Uzbek bread, *lavosh*, flat and round, baked in a wood-fired oven. I discussed American pumpkins with the elderly woman who sold me roasted pumpkin seeds. The cheese lady with the purple eye shadow gave me a sample of the cheese she recommended this week. I saw the arrival of the latest harvest: fresh peas, radishes, beets, and new potatoes. Two young girls walked by, each carrying one side of a basket that contained four puppies. I searched the market for a soccer shirt, a *futbolka*, for my son and a fur hat with ear flaps for my daughter. What do I think of this place?

"*I like this place very much,*" I tell the peanut lady.

She pours the measure of nuts into a plastic bag, adds a few extra for good measure. I hand her the coins. "*Life is hard here, isn't it?*" she says.

"Yes, it is. But the people seem happy."

The peanut lady likes that answer; she tells me to come back to buy from her another time, and I continue on my way to my apartment. If my Russian skills allowed, I would tell her that there is a captivating grace about life in this quiet provincial city.

"Why don't Americans ever have any time?" Max, a student at the university, asks me. "Whenever I invite the Peace Corps volunteer Bill to come for a walk, he always says he doesn't have time."

The guidebook spends one page on the city of Poltava, population 350,000, and another on the Poltava region. It mentions two museums, one church, and a battlefield. Poltava isn't a flashy place. Much of the architecture, apart from the buildings on the main street, is Khrushchev-style Soviet, large concrete apartment buildings with dilapidated balconies, apparently designed for hanging laundry. Poltava University is also from this utilitarian period of Soviet architecture. On the roof in enormous letters is a simple sign—*Universityet*. Billboards with straightforward messages line the roads.

On the other hand, in Times Square, lights flashing, goods and entertainment in abundance at every turn, countless restaurants, theaters, and shops, I'm not sure people enjoy themselves more than in Poltava. In Times Square, they are definitely spending more money, and we Americans seem to equate pleasure with spending money.

Here in Poltava, the residents stroll down October Street arm in arm without buying anything more than some black sunflower seeds in a cone of rolled-up newspaper.

"Dasha and I are going for a walk," my friend Natasha says over the phone. She works as an English translator. "Would you like to join us?"

This is a familiar walk. We start at the park in the center, where there is a stark cylindrical monument dedicated to Peter the Great for his defeat of the Swedish invaders in 1709 at the Battle of Poltava. This monument, not a thing of beauty to my mind, is the symbol of Poltava for Ukrainians. A bride and groom are posing for photographs in front of this single black column just as bridal parties did four years ago, and probably for generations before that. The new crop of toddlers is circling the monument in the battery-operated cars, rented from the photographers who congregate at this spot. The benches are filled with people, young and old, sitting, talking, drinking beer, watching passersby.

At the end of the park, we cross the street by descending into the new glass-enclosed underpass and come back up on the pedestrian avenue in front of a lady playing an accordion and another selling bouquets of tiny blue bachelor buttons. We stroll along the cobblestoned street, past the slightly wilted splendor of the Gogol Theater, the chocolate shops, two more parks with fountains, the music academy, and the new white church with the gold dome. At the end of October Street we join other pedestrians at the white arched monument, and we all look down into the lower part of the city. Everyone who lives in Poltava has taken this walk, seen this monument, looked at this view innumerable times, but people are still drawn to the south end of October Street. Students, who have been partying all night in celebration of their graduation, inevitably wind up at this white monument to watch the sun rise. I've never heard anyone say, "There's nowhere to go in this town. It's always the same walk, the same view, the same old monument."

The guidebook concedes that Poltava has a long cultural tradition. Gogol was born in this region, as were Shalom Aleichem,

Kotlarevsky, and other poets and musicians less known to us in the West. There are several museums and theaters, a puppet theater, a few cinemas, and a stadium, home to a professional football (soccer) team. Monuments mark nearly every important intersection, and stately chestnut trees line the avenues. The city is famous, at least among its inhabitants, for its parks, including the large Victory Park with a rickety Ferris wheel and a tiny roller coaster, called *Amerikanskye gora*, American Mountains. But somehow the litany of attractions doesn't create an accurate picture of the gentle life of this town.

Natasha, ten year-old Dasha, and I backtrack and turn into a park in front of the regional museum. There is an enormous statue of Lenin in the square that retains his name.

"There aren't any monuments to Stalin or Trotsky anymore," Natasha says, "but Lenin had some important ideas."

A few blocks more and we come to my favorite park, White Birch Square, a small common with many birch trees and some flower beds. The grass, as in all the parks of Poltava, is unmowed and wild. No one tries to control crab grass or dandelions. In the center of the square is a bust of Pushkin. Surrounding the park are well-maintained apartment buildings; it feels a bit like Paris here, only seedier. Children are kicking around a soccer ball among the birches. Friends or lovers sit on benches talking. That's what people seem to do in Poltava; they walk together and they talk. They take pleasure in each other's company.

I leave Dasha and Natasha at the entrance to their street, and crossing the central park, I head back toward the university. Around some benches, a large group of pensioners has gathered; a gray-haired woman plays the accordion and sings in a strong voice. I recognize her from a photo my husband Frank took four years ago when she was also singing and playing at this same spot. The pensioners gather here every weekend. Men and women harmonize at full voice in a minor key; many others dance on the pavement. Everyone can sing and dance in Ukraine; men and women, or women and women, waltz together to the accordion and to the vocal accompaniment. The musician strikes up a different tune; the seniors choose new partners or stay with the old ones and begin again, laughing and singing as they dance. I know these people barely have enough to subsist on, but their poverty doesn't seem to keep them from dancing here, year after year.

Two teenagers in jeans stroll by with their arms around each other. On other evenings, this same spot is a site of karaoke, which also draws a big crowd of the younger set.

As the accordion strikes up a waltz, the young man pulls the girl to him, and unselfconsciously they join in, fifty pensioners and two teenagers, dancing in the open air under the chestnut trees.

The next day, my phone rings. It is Natasha. "We're going to take a walk," she says. "Would you like to join us?" What a good idea; we can walk down October Street. Maybe we'll go to the white monument and look at the view.

Sailor, Vladivostok, Russian Far East. 2008

To Russia

What is this compulsion with the Russian language? I have endured three years of impossible Russian classes at Mount Holyoke and Amherst Colleges, staying up past midnight with endless noun declensions, fighting acrobatic pronunciation and swallowing the humiliation of illiteracy. I must be a bit mad. Maybe anyone who presses on with the Russian language is mad. Each of my American Russian teachers seems to be, in his or her own way, snared by this obsessive language and the wealth of literature that it has created, by its depth and the extravagance of misery and joy it communicates.

When the new semester starts, I go running to my previous Russian professor Susan Downing to complain of the difficulties of third year Russian.

"I can't do it," I say. "I have to translate every word. I don't know enough grammar. It's too hard."

"Everyone hits the wall with third year Russian," she says. "You never feel you know enough grammar."

"The Russians have suffered so much," I say. We have just read Akhmatova's "Requiem," with its image of the women walking the prison line, waiting for the opportunity to bring home-cooked food to their sons or husbands or lovers. "The tsars, the Revolution, the Civil War, the loss of a way of life again and again, the bitter winters, Stalin's terrors, the prison camps, exile, genocide, world war."

Susan nods. "You're hooked," she says.

And so I am.

I apply for a Fulbright Senior Scholars grant to do English teacher training in Russia. I am assigned to Irkutsk State Linguistic University, five thousand kilometers from Moscow, deep in Siberia. My photographer husband will join me on the journey. He will deposit me at my destination, stay for ten days, and then fly back to Massachusetts to fulfill his teaching obligations for the semester.

Irkutsk station, Siberia. 2008

Trans-Siberian

The Ukrainians must win the prize for hospitality. As soon as Svetlana, my friend and colleague from Ukraine, hears that Frank and I will arrive in Moscow, she arranges for us to stay in the home of her ex-daughter-in-law Irina and grandson Sasha. Svetlana travels on the overnight train from Poltava, a trip of eighteen hours, to meet us at the Moscow airport. We sleep in Irina's living room, also Sasha's bedroom. Svetlana, Sasha, and Irina all sleep in the remaining room. For the two days that we are in Moscow, Irina arranges for her relatives to drive us everywhere, and Svetlana dedicates all her time to our needs. First is the requisite visit to Red Square to see the wildly ornate St. Basel's Church and to prove that we are truly in Moscow. Then she helps us change money and accompanies us to the Fulbright Office to move the boxes of books I shipped from Massachusetts to the train station for storage until we depart. Our second night in Moscow, we are feted by Irina's uncle Slava. As the honored guests, hosted and toasted, we get a tour of every corner of Slava's new home. We even see the phone in his daughter's shower.

We must leave Moscow within seventy-two hours, before it is required that we register with the Moscow police. Irina enlists another friend Dima to drive us to the train station at midnight. It is bitter cold, and Dima is wearing thin-soled pointy-toed city shoes. He stamps his feet on the concrete to keep them from freezing, but none of them would consider leaving before the train departs. Four people stuff Frank and me and our 240 pounds of baggage into our first-class sleeping compartment. Irina hands us a box of chocolates. Dima, whom we have never met before, kisses Frank and me on both cheeks. I think if she could, Svetlana would accompany us for seventy-eight hours, four nights and three days on that train just to make sure everyone treats us well. I see her speaking to the conductor in charge of our compartment, the *provodnika*, probably warning her that her head will be on the chopping block if she doesn't take good care of us.

So here we are, two narrow berths with clean sheets, a table in between. Pop music is being piped through a speaker over our heads. Behind the curtain, frigid air coats the bottom of the window with a layer of ice, but it's hot in the airless compartment. Svetlana has equipped us with a satchel of salami, brown bread, cucumbers, and a bottle of vodka. We put the provisions up against the window to keep the food cold. We could start the journey drinking vodka, but a long trip lies ahead, and the train wheels lull us with a steady rhythm into the night.

In the morning, it's apparent the first-class car, with its high-priced berths, is nearly empty; of the nine double compartments, only two, besides our own, are occupied. We see our neighbors only occasionally fleeing down the corridor, on the right a long-legged blond beauty, dressed for the hothouse environment of the train, in very short shorts and a tiny top. On the left a heavy-set man with no shirt at all and a hairy back. The third class cars, with their dormitory-style sleeping accommodations, are jammed full of school children returning from their winter vacation camps. The *provodnika* informs us, as a stream of chattering kids runs through the compartment, that there are 250 children on the train traveling without their parents, and since they will be eating in the dining car, there won't be any room for us to eat there. At mid-morning, a member of the restaurant staff brings what could be called breakfast to our compartment, a chicken leg and potatoes in a Styrofoam box, a small container of strawberry yogurt, a chocolate bar, and a Choco-pie. It doesn't really matter what meal they call this since we are barreling forward into future time zones and are still jet lagged from past ones.

I finally understand I am far, far from home when I step off the train onto the platform in a town several hours east of Moscow. It's only 3 PM, but dusk is falling, and it's no more than 5°F. The hawkers on the platforms are bundled in mittens, mufflers, hats and hoods, long coats, boots. They wave cheap stuffed animals to the passengers in the windows, many of whom come rushing out from other cars into the cold in their slippers and pajama pants to make purchases. As soon as I step off the overheated train, a round lady waves to me and gingerly makes her way across the icy platform, swinging a plastic tote bag.

"*Pirozhi?*" She pulls aside a corner of the cloth napkin that covers her bag. Steam is released from the pile of stuffed fried dumplings.

I shake my head, too shy to make the purchase. Maybe tomorrow I will feel braver.

The train starts up again past simple wood houses buried in snow. Yards are filled with refuse. Each plot has a miserable outhouse, and I see hand pumps, signs of obligatory trips into the freezing cold. Many industrial sites are abandoned, either never completed or no longer functioning. Heavy machinery sits rusting and unused. Citizens haul their tote bags along icy paths, their shoulders hunched against the wind.

Twenty hours from Moscow is the city of Perm, the site of an infamous gulag, functioning until 1988. Perm-36 was a slave labor camp, where men, exiled for untold arbitrary reasons, died of starvation and overwork.

From the comfort of the first class compartment, we look out at the hoar frost covering the forests and fields. Miles and miles pass before us. The pine forest changes to birch. Siberia officially begins twenty-four hours from Moscow with the Ural Mountains. In the middle of the second night the train stops in Yekaterinburg, remote and forbidding, where the Romanovs were sent to exile and then executed. We are less than one-third of the way to our destination.

On the second day, when the hawkers come to the windows to show their smoked fish, I pull on my boots, down coat, and fur hat and foray out. The air instantly penetrates my face and lungs. Large round golden fish are splayed out, spine and bones on one flat side, skin on the other. I choose the vendor that all the other passengers are crowding. With a look at the train to be sure it isn't starting to move and with a minimum of words (*"This, please. How much?"*), I manage to escape back to the warmth of the train compartment clutching my catch in a plastic bag. The train lurches forward. Frank eagerly unwraps the moon-shaped fish. It has a tantalizing smoky smell, but the first greasy fork yields a mouthful of tiny bones.

Frank hangs the fish from the shade in the compartment window and photographs it, the daylight shining though the translucent flesh, lace curtains on either side, and the vodka bottle below. Before bed that evening, with the compartment smelling like the neighborhood deli, we throw the fish in the trash bin at the end of the car. The train carries us deeper and deeper.

Expedition, Angara River, Siberia. 2008

Cold in Irkutsk

In Massachusetts when the temperature goes below zero for an extended period, two weeks would be considered an eternity-things start to go haywire. The car doors freeze shut, and their batteries die; the furnace pumps constantly, but still the basement needs additional light bulbs to keep the pipes from freezing. Sometimes the oil freezes on its way to the furnace; then we defrost it with a hair dryer. Once the drainpipes froze in the basement, and the toilets backed up. A siege mentality prevails; no one wants to leave the house for very long. That's at 0°F, approximately -18°C.

That's a warm day here in Irkutsk. *Tiepló*, they would say. Today it is -32°C/-23°F, colder than we have ever seen in Massachusetts. Perhaps it should have been obvious to me, but I didn't anticipate how much the cold would dominate every aspect of living here in January.

In Irkutsk, people don't have cars to protect them from the cold. Waiting for the bus takes on heroic proportions. The public transportation consists of rattletrap buses and trolleys and small private vans called *marshrutkis* that circle the city on prescribed routes. As soon as anyone gets to the street, the primary goal is to get into a *marshrutka* as quickly as possible. When one arrives at the stop, there is a crowd surge to the door. The people who cannot fit in are left to freeze while they wait for the next opportunity. Once a person is lucky enough to get a seat in a *marshrutka* or has settled for the big squeeze of the bus or trolley, the windows of the vehicle are so frozen that it is impossible to see outside. Of course, the driver doesn't announce the name of the stop. Passengers constantly ask each other, *"Where are we? What stop is this?"* One young woman demonstrates how I should make a hole in the ice on the window to see where I am. She removes her glove and warms the window with her bare hand until the ice defrosts. I should have brought a car scraper. I would be the hero of the bus.

Frank likes to photograph in the early and late light, so every morning we bundle up to face the most severe cold of the day. We explore some new part of the city: the riverfront, the train station, the area below the dam. My long down coat protects my core, but we seem to have a tolerance of about two hours before the nose, the cheeks, the fingers, and the toes start to burn. Each day we experiment to find an optimum combination of layers, one day two pairs of wool socks, the next day a second pair of long johns. The fashionable ladies of Irkutsk may walk around town in their stiletto boots, but yesterday I gave up and pulled my clunky Sorels over two pairs of socks. Every day I look more and more like one of the old women on the street, the *babushki*, scarf under my hat, lumbering across the icy streets with my tote bag of bread, milk and eggs.

It is -36°C/-33°F on the day we go to the Chinese market, a street where immigrants set up their outdoor stalls of knock-off clothing and household goods. We are searching for a few items to make my dorm apartment more comfortable: dish towels, pot holders, an egg carrier. We toy with the idea of installing a toilet seat as a donation to the university. The faces of the vendors peering out from layers of insulated coats and hoods are East or Central Asian. Men and women alike wear massive boots of felt or fur. One vendor has plastic bags wrapped around her feet.

"*I'm from Azerbaijan,*" says the man from whom I purchase two soup spoons, a grater, and two forks to complement the two bent ones in the kitchen. He tries to entice me to add a shot glass or two.

"*I'm Kyrgyz,*" his neighbor says. "*We don't drink vodka.*"

"*Do you stand out here all day?*" I ask. My toes are aching after one hour.

"*All day,*" they say. "*What to do?*"

At the back of the market, a grimy restaurant proclaims itself in both Vietnamese and Russian script. It is so painfully cold, I can't stop thinking about a bowl of steaming Vietnamese *pho*, but the place looks as if I might regret it for many days to come.

Although there are still several items on my list, we have to escape the cold. As we pick up speed, trying to get back to the bus stop, the concrete paths seem to radiate more cold than the wooden walks or even the ice on the frozen ground.

We pass a dog standing on three feet with one paw raised for some relief from the cold ground. Then that paw goes down and another paw is raised.

"The three-legged dogs of Irkutsk," Frank says.

Back at the apartment, I unpack my meager purchases. All the food I left in my refrigerator is frozen. The cabbage, the only vegetable I had found in the neighborhood supermarket, is solid ice.

Later, at the university, we discuss the upcoming excursion to Lake Baikal on Saturday.

"It is supposed to be cold in the next few days. It always gets cold for the holiday of Epiphany," Olga says. She will be our guide for the trip.

"As cold as today?" I say.

"Oh no. Much colder."

Julia in her dorm, Irkutsk, Siberia. 2008

Dormitory Life

The corridors, lobbies, and elevators of every apartment building I have seen in Russia are dilapidated, literally coming apart. The plaster is falling off; the paint is peeling, floor tiles missing, stairs broken and uneven. There are often no lights in the corridors or in the elevators. Perhaps there is no budget for maintenance, or perhaps there's no interest. Or maybe this neglect is a remnant of the Soviet Union. Like any collective, the corridor and lobby belong to no one, and no one cares about them.

This neglect is especially apparent in the university dormitory. The Vice Rector told me that the university replaced the windows of the main buildings, located on the central square of the city, but there was no money to maintain the dorms, a couple of kilometers out of the center.

There are four dorms, Khrushchev-style block apartment buildings. I live in Building Four on the fourth floor. There are no outside lights despite a buildup of ice on the front step. The entryway is also dark. Russians seem to be obsessed with crowd control, so means of egress are always restricted. There are two staircases in the building; I can descend all the way to street level via the staircase immediately outside my door, but when I get to the bottom, a barred gate, sealed with an enormous padlock blocks my exit. I guess this is not a litigious society. A university in the US would be sued if anyone fell on the ice or had difficulty getting out of a building in an emergency. I'm glad there's an enormous fire hose on the wall in my apartment, assuming it works.

Before I arrived, I was in communication with Tatiana from the International Relations Office at the university. She said the university could provide me with housing in a faculty apartment in the student dormitory at no charge. When I worked in Ukraine, I had a comfortable little apartment in the student dormitory. Of course it had some problems, specifically no hot water or no water at all at random times, but I remember being quite satisfied. So I informed Tatiana that I would try living in the dorm.

I knew it would be a communal apartment this time, so I envisioned what I had seen in Ukraine, faculty living in the dorm on a relatively permanent basis, sharing a kitchen, bath, and WC, but each person with relative privacy for eating, sleeping, and entertaining.

It was one of the coldest days of the winter when we arrived. We had to climb four flights of stairs, hauling my one hundred pounds of luggage, Frank's forty pounds, and the one hundred pounds of books that I had shipped to the Fulbright office in Moscow and transported on the trans-Siberian train. The crumbling blue corridors reminded me of the projects in the ghetto. The floors were a mixture of wood and broken linoleum. The student WCs on each floor had no doors on the stalls and smelled of illicit cigarettes and urine.

We were ushered into a faculty apartment where some guest teachers from the environs of Irkutsk were temporarily housed, sharing three of the four bedrooms. My room was the last on the hall at the outer edge of the building. We could immediately tell that it was much too cold. The balcony door didn't close properly, and it was -30°C/-22°F outside.

There's a reason why *nye rabotaet* (It doesn't work) is the first thing we learn in Russian. We had to stick plastic bags around the cracks of the balcony door. The TV was broken. The closet door had fallen off its runners. I kept tripping on the holes in the lino-leum floor. The light bulbs flickered off at random. The balcony overlooked a humming power station.

Now those first depressing days are in the past. As soon as the visiting teachers departed, I went to the *dezhurnaya*, the lady who guards the front door. *"I'm all alone here,"* I said in Russian. *"Why can't I have my very favorite room?"* But she wouldn't let me see the other rooms, so I got the dean to call. She ordered the *dezhurnaya* to let me have my choice of rooms in the apartment. I moved to a room with interior walls. It was 6°F warmer than the corner room. I cannibalized all the other rooms for the best TV, the best refrig-erator, the best desks, the best pillows, and the best mattresses.

Frank is back in the States, and there's no one here but me now. My clothesline is hanging in the bathroom. I bought a tea-pot, a cutting board, a dish drainer, a sharp knife, and some mugs. I don't keep them in my room; they are in their proper place in the kitchen. I leave my bedroom door open, instead of closing it like a hotel room. There's food in the kitchen cupboard, soap and shampoo in the shower room, and toilet paper in the WC. It looks like someone lives here, albeit very simply. I'm thinking of splurging for a toilet seat.

"Don't buy a toilet seat," my Russian teacher in the US writes me. "Someone will steal it!"

Of course, I can't do anything about the power station out-side my window or the crumbling dormitory corridors, but in my apartment there's a pot of tea on the stove, clementines, dried kumquats, and fish smoked at Lake Baikal in the fridge. I've been growing sprouts and eating them with fresh rye bread and cheese everyday, and I've found Chinese cabbage in the central market. Pictures of friends and family are taped on the wall. The radiator is warm, and the TV shows Russian soap operas. One night I watched the old classic *Potemkin*.

Then, one day, after my trip to the university, I walk into the apartment and can immediately tell something is different. My shoes left in the hall are piled up in a corner. The ironing board is closed. My dish drainer sits on the counter instead of in the sink where I left it. The sprouts have been moved from one counter to another. My bedroom, however, which I always lock when I leave, seems to be undisturbed.

I rush down to the *dezhurnaya*. "*Is someone else moving into my apartment?*" I know it can happen, but it feels like my apartment now.

"*No, we just came in and cleaned.*"

Eight in the evening, I hear the lock being opened. No knock on the door, just someone walking into the apartment as if it is public space. It is the *dezhurnaya*. I waylay her between the kitchen and bathroom.

"*I just came to see if the apartment is clean,*" she says.

"*Yes, it's fine, thank you.*"

She tries to peer into my bedroom, but I stand in the way. Then she enters the kitchen and goes directly to the sprouts. "*What are these?*"

Maybe the cleaning lady told her about the sprouts and the *dezhurnaya* is here to see them for herself. I can imagine the report. "*That gray-haired American lady has soft toilet paper and fancy soap. She's filtering water, and something is growing in the kitchen.*"

"*This is my garden,*" I say. "*They're radish seeds. Taste them.*"

She tries one sprout and then another and another. She starts to laugh. "*Tasty,*" she says.

"*And healthy,*" I say.

She handles my herbal teas. She looks at the vitamins I brought from the US. *"And is your hair natural?"* she says. Her hair is a purplish red, but her face isn't young.

"I'm sixty years old," I say.

"Me too," she says.

"In America, some women leave their hair a natural color. It's easier."

"It looks good," she says.

I give her an envelope with some radish seeds and explain how to sprout them.

"You're all set up here," she says.

Either things have improved, or my expectations have diminished. Maybe someday I'll buy a rug or a table lamp. There's still no toilet seat, but I measured the width of the toilet with a piece of string, and I keep the string in my bag just in case I happen to see a toilet seat for sale.

Subway, Moscow. 2008

Tea Party

Irkutsk, evidently, is not Ukraine. I have been here since January 14, and not one person has tried to make contact with me outside of work. After feeling sorry for myself for a while, I decide to take a lesson from my Ukrainian friends.

"I would like to invite you and Valia and Larisa to tea at my apartment," I tell Olga. "I want to hear about your classes." These are three young English teachers from the American Studies Department. I will model teaching techniques in their classes. Olga is a petite blonde who wears a mink hat with rhinestones. Valia is a sporty-looking dark-eyed young woman in jeans and hiking boots. I haven't met Larisa yet. They all teach on Saturdays, but they will be free after 11:30 AM, and they seem to be thrilled to be invited.

These will be my first visitors. I've attended enough Ukrainian lunches and dinners to know how to do this. Tea really means as much as you can possibly eat. These young ladies will be hungry after teaching just as I always am after standing in front of a class. So we'll call it tea, but I'll just make a few salads and serve some sliced meat, fish, and cheese with brown bread. We can make those open-faced sandwiches, *buterbrodi* they call them.

This is a big deal for me, my only social event since I arrived in Irkutsk. Three guests is a stretch for my minimally equipped kitchen. I wash the floor with the rag that the cleaning lady left drying on my bathroom radiator. I set up the second bed in my room as a couch, placing pillows along the wall and covering everything with a blanket. I make my shopping list.

Ever since I discovered the food in the central market, the starvation days of the frozen cabbage are over. One of the distinguishing characteristics of the Irkutsk indoor market is the wide variety of smoked fish and caviar. Here the fish comes from Lake Baikal; there isn't any worry about it being caught downstream from Chernobyl, as in Ukraine. The fish lady is always happy to see me because I buy fillets, more expensive than the whole bony fish. I learned my lesson after purchasing that fish from the lady at the station during our train ride.

The Irkutsk market has a section of prepared salads, sold by the hundred grams, transported home in plastic bags: cabbage salad, beet salad, pickled wild mushrooms. There is also *kimchi* for an exorbitant price and something that I would swear is a form of dried tofu. I'll have to ask the Chinese students in my Russian class. But I'm not in the market for prepared salads today. I'm going to make my own.

Ethnic Buriyat women line up to sell their homemade farmer cheese and sour cream. They hawk their wares by offering a sample. Next to them are brined pickles by the piece or by the jar and cooked hams and sausages. Anything can be sampled on request.

But I head for the produce. When it comes to fresh fruits and vegetables, this is not among the great markets of the world. It isn't Oaxaca or Istanbul or even Stop and Shop back home, but there is a respectable assortment for prices that are comparable to, or higher than, prices in the US. That would be excessive for the Russian teachers at the university. They tell me they mostly shop on the street where the prices are lower. The food on the street is quite dog-eared and may be three-quarters frozen. Persimmons and currants seem to be sold completely frozen. I wonder what they do with frozen persimmons.

I select a red pepper, some scallions, carrots, and parsley and splurge on a tomato. Cucumbers are about seven dollars a kilo, so I pass on them. Who knows where this produce originates at this time of year? The most extravagant purchase is some good-looking leaf lettuce sold by the kilo. I ask for half a kilo, so the merchant takes a cleaver and chops the lettuce in half. That half lettuce sets me back about four dollars.

The spice vendors are usually Kyrgyz or Uzbek. They don't write the names of the spices displayed in wooden compartmentalized trays. The merchants make their own spice blends with no list of ingredients, just what the combination is used for. This mixture is good for shish kabob, that one for *borscht*; another is for soup. The customers seem to use the spice vendors like doctors. *"Please give me something good for shashlik."* This doesn't help me much. I am looking for caraway seeds, my secret ingredient in cole slaw. I wish I had looked up the word for "caraway" before going to the market. I ask to taste a couple of types of seeds that look like they might be caraway, and I settle for some approximation.

Outside I stop at one of the stands for three more forks since my kitchen only has two that aren't bent. It is not possible to buy flat table knives. I pause to admire the puppies for sale. The day is mild by Siberian standards, a sweltering +2°F, so the breeders have brought their puppies out: poodles, German shepherds, Dobermans. They are swaddled in blankets and piled together in boxes to keep them warm. A purebred puppy costs about sixty dollars.

Back in the apartment, I prepare three salads, an egg salad, my generally acclaimed cole slaw, and a lettuce salad with tomatoes, peppers, and scallions. I don't have the ingredients for my usual house dressing, so I concoct something with *kefir* and mustard and garlic. It tastes pretty good. The seeds in the cole slaw are definitely not caraway after all. They give the slaw a nasty bitter taste, so I try to cut it with more sugar, oil, and mayonnaise.

The young ladies arrive carrying a pink cake decorated with maraschino cherries.

Valia admires my apartment. "Wonderful," she says. She lived in the dorm of the university when she was a student.

Lunch is a great success. We sit in the kitchen, eating and talking for three hours. They eat every bit. Little Olga wolfs down the smoked fish. Valia polishes off the egg salad. Larisa declares that eating a green salad makes her feel that it is summer. They all love the herbal teas from the States. No one but me seems to mind the bitter flavor in the cole slaw.

"You are a wonderful hostess," Olga says.

I guess I have learned something from my Ukrainian friends.

In the last few days there seems to be a change in Irkutsk. Irina Fyodorovna, the chair of American Studies, says that winter is almost over, but it's early February; you can't fool me. Even at home in Ashfield the snow won't melt until the end of March. Still, here in Irkutsk, we haven't seen -36°C/-33°F for a while. Now the morning temperatures are a balmy -22°C/-8°F.

Perhaps people's molecules are beginning to stir just a little. Tatiana from the International Relations Office wants to meet me for tea someday. We make a date for Sunday; then she postpones it. The students in Olga's class say they want to go skating with me, but we'll need to wait until the temperature rises above -10°C/15°F so the softy from the US doesn't freeze her eyeballs.

Dariya, one of the teachers in the American Studies program, hears that I have a ticket to the ballet tonight. "Are you going alone?" she asks.

I shrug my shoulders. "That's the way it is here," I say.

"I would like to go to the theater with you," she says. "Someday."
Maybe it has just been too cold for a social life in Siberia.

Ice swimming, Lake Baikal, Siberia. 2008

An Invitation

When I enter the dormitory, an older woman is talking through the window into the room where the *dezhurnaya* sits. I wait to ask the *dezhurnaya* if there has been any progress in replacing my electric kettle which stopped working a couple of days ago.

The older woman listens to my Russian conversation, and then she follows me down the hall. "Do you speak English?" she calls after me. "Where are you from? And from which state?"

She introduces herself as Nataliya, a member of the translation faculty at the university. She is tall, with a long wrinkled face, a deep voice, and a deliberate manner of speaking English. She lives on the fifth floor of the dormitory. Her husband was abusive, she says, so she had to move into the dormitory.

"Many Russians don't like Americans," she says, "because they are quite arrogant. They think their way is better."

I don't respond, but I know that I am often guilty of this.

"But I think that when the Soviet Union was destroyed, America was spared because it has a spiritual power. You are Protestants," she says.

"Some are," I say.

"More than sixty-five percent are Protestant," Nataliya says. "And an even higher percent are believers. Are you Protestant?"

"No, I'm not."

"Do you mean to tell me that you are not a believer?"

"I guess you could say that. I consider myself a Buddhist."

"Oh, well that's fine," Nataliya says. "I myself am Lutheran, but I can go to any church. I believe in reincarnation. There is a spiritual revival occurring in Siberia; some say it is centered to the west, nearer Novosibirsk. But those places are spiritually dirty."

This bizarre conversation is taking place as we walk up the stairs. When we get to my floor, the fourth, I pause in the doorway to the corridor.

"And are you initiated?" she asks. "Do you know Shambala? Have you been to Tibet?"

I feel like the ghost of Madame Blavatsky has pursued me up the stairs. It must be my American reticence to talk about religious beliefs with strangers, but I keep trying to back away to evade her questions. And what are the answers to her questions? There hasn't been a person in Irkutsk who has shown any personal interest in me. I would like to see the Siberian world of the *banya* on the lake side, the shamans, and the surviving Buddhist sites. This is the first person who has intimated that a world exists here, other than the marketplace and the ruins of the Soviet Union. Yet, I just want to escape down the corridor and into my apartment.

"Do you have visions?" she asks leaning her face very close to mine. "Or perhaps I shouldn't ask."

I suppose I could just say no and end the conversation, but I know that this region and the areas to the east, south, and north have a history of Buddhism and shamanism that predates the Soviet Union. People in this area of all religious persuasions consider Lake Baikal a sacred place.

"I went to Lake Baikal," I say. "And I saw the people bathing in the icy water for the Epiphany. That night I had a dream that I also jumped in the water. It wasn't terrible; in fact, I liked it."

"That was not a dream," Nataliya says. "It was real."

I race down the corridor and slam the door of my apartment behind me.

I am soaking in the bathtub that evening when the phone rings. When I first arrived, the *dezhurnaya* told me that it didn't work, but it rings every night, usually while I am in the tub. It is always the wrong number, so I have given up answering it. Anyone who needs to call me can use my cell number.

One night when the phone rang and I answered, the man on the other end could tell from my *hello* that I was an English speaker, so he asked in English to speak to Viktoria.

"You have the wrong number," I said.

"I'm sorry."

"Now, could you please tell me how to say 'You have the wrong number' in Russian?"

"I have understood you," he said.

"But I would like you to tell me how to answer the telephone *po-russkie*. I want to tell people they have dialed wrong."

So he told me, "*Vi ashiblis nomerom*," and I repeated it a couple of times.

"Thank you," I said.

"Good luck."

I wrote the new expression on a paper by the phone, but I haven't used it. It seems that my phone rings somewhere else in this dormitory also. When it rings in my apartment, I hear someone nearby running. If I pick up the receiver on the third or fourth ring, people are talking in Italian. So, my theory is that there is an Italian girl, probably Viktoria, who lives next door or upstairs. She gets phone calls from home nearly every night, and because of some mysterious Russian wiring, our two phones are on the same line. Either it's a mistake, or it's one of the old party lines such as we used to have in Ashfield when we first moved in.

I'm just as happy not to answer. Phone conversations in a second language are very difficult. There are no visual cues to help with comprehension.

I arrived in Irkutsk with a yellow index card with two names on it, Anastasia Michaelovna and Galina Sergeyevna. Next to the names were two telephone numbers. My Ukrainian friends Lyuda and Ganna in the US had given me these names. Lyuda had told me that the mother of her friend from Ukraine was living in Irkutsk. My understanding was that Galina, the mother of Anastasia, Lyuda's friend in Ukraine, was a teacher of Russian in Irkutsk; however, I don't get everything straight since Lyuda and I talk half the time in Russian and half in English, so we can both practice.

Now in Irkutsk, it has taken me nearly a month of speaking in Russian before I attempt to talk on the phone to this mother of Lyuda's friend. This might be an awkward call to make even in English, but in Russian, changing all those nouns and adjectives for six cases, three genders, singular and plural, while talking into a machine, is a killer.

Finally, I steel myself and call. *"May I please speak to Galina Sergeyevna?"* Even that sentence isn't straightforward because I need the instrumental case in Russian. Fortunately, it is Galina Sergeyevna who answers, so I explain who I am. *"Your daughter Anastasia in Ukraine is a friend of my friend Lyuda in America* (two nominative case nouns, a genitive case and two prepositional cases)."

Well, unfortunately, Galina doesn't have a daughter Anastasia (genitive case) or any daughter at all, but she has a son (nominative case). There is an Anastasia (nominative case), but she doesn't live in Ukraine (prepositional case); she lives in Irkutsk now (prepositional case). Anastasia is Galina's sister (genitive case). So who is Anastasia's mother (genitive case), the person I am trying to talk to? And is Anastasia's mother (genitive case) a teacher (nominative case) of Russian? (prepositional or is it accusative or genitive?) Now I am totally confused, and so is the poor woman I am talking with. In the end it turns out that Anastasia is a woman in her sixties (dative case), and it is Anastasia's daughter, whose name I never learn, who lives in Ukraine. That daughter with no name must be Lyuda's friend, so maybe it is Anastasia that I want to talk to.

"*And why are you calling?*" Galina asks.

That is a hard question to answer, both for its grammar and its content.

"*Well, I don't know anyone* (genitive case or is it accusative?) *in Irkutsk* (prepositional case), *and I was hoping I could meet your family* (instrumental case)." It's difficult to invite yourself into someone's home or life, especially using the conditional verbs and the instrumental case in Russian.

By the time the conversation is over, I am thoroughly exhausted. Galina urges me to call her sister, but it takes me a week to dare to make another phone call.

This time I call Anastasia's number. She knows who I am right away. She has been expecting my call. "*And why didn't you call sooner?*" she says.

Ah, well . . .

"*I'm so glad to hear from you,*" she says. "*When can we meet? I would like to invite you to have some traditional Russian food.*" My first actual invitation in Irkutsk.

We arrange to meet the next day at the university in front of the internet café, my favorite haunt.

"And how will I know you?" Anastasia asks.

"Oh, you won't have any trouble. No one else does." I'm the one with the strange hair, as one of the students told me.

Anastasia, a handsome woman in a long coat, is immediately on informal terms. She uses the *ti* instead of the *vi* to address me. As we walk across the street, she takes my arm and starts to tell me the story of her life. Her Russian is quite understandable, but every once in a while she asks me if I understand. Born in Irkutsk, she lived thirty years in Ukraine. After the death of two husbands, she has returned in the last few months to her hometown to care for her ailing father and invalid sister. Her three daughters and four grandchildren are divided between Ukraine and Irkutsk.

"So, where is your heart?" I ask.

She pauses for a moment. *"Here in the town of my birth,"* she says.

Across the square is a little cafeteria that specializes in *blini*, which Russians translate as pancakes, but they are blintzes to me, stuffed with farmer cheese, rolled, with a small dollop of sour cream on top, very similar to the ones of my childhood. Anastasia orders *blini* and a plate of *pilmeni* for each of us. *Pilmeni* are considered the regional food of Siberia. Every culture has their version, ravioli in Italy or won tons in China or momos in Tibet. Ukrainian *vereniki* are larger than these *pilmeni*, which contain meat and are served quite unaccompanied on a plate. The food is delicious, fresh and simple. Anastasia won't allow me to pay. *"You are the guest,"* she says.

I'm especially sorry I can't cover the bill when she explains during the course of the meal that she is currently re-applying for Russian citizenship, and although she worked for thirty years in Ukraine, not as a Russian teacher by the way, she has neither a Ukrainian pension nor a Russian one until she receives her

Russian passport again. Even then her pension will only be about $160 a month. At the moment, the rest of the family is helping her financially.

Over tea, I show her my family and home photos and give her a picture of Lyuda and Ganna in the US. I finally have the opportunity to use one of the many gifts I have brought from the US, a tea towel printed with a New England scene and a calendar. It has a dowel so it can be hung on the wall as a calendar for the year, and then it can be converted into a towel.

Anastasia has many ideas for excursions we can make together, to the theater, to Lake Baikal in the spring. She says her father is ill, so she doesn't feel comfortable inviting me to her home. I suggest she accompany me to the ballet.

"*We'll have to see how much the tickets cost,*" she says.

"*I am inviting you. You will be my guest,*" I say.

At first she is doubtful; then she accepts.

We walk back to the *marshrutka* minivan stop, where we say goodbye with a hug. I smile all the way home on the *marshrutka* even if everyone stares at me. It isn't the Russian custom to smile for no apparent reason.

I have another connection to a person in Irkutsk. This one is even more remote. I have the name and address of a friend of a friend of a friend; I've seen his picture via email. He has a big bushy beard and looks quite like the Siberian woodsman. This man Stanislav lives right down Lenin Street close to the university, but I don't have a phone number. Do I dare knock on his door?

Cleaning carpets, Lake Baikal, Siberia. 2008

Communal Living

Despite two massive fires, many traditional Siberian wooden houses remain standing in Irkutsk complete with their carved latticework and peeling paint. At night an acrid smell of smoke hangs over these traditional neighborhoods. I don't know what they are burning for heating fuel, but it smells toxic. Each house seems to have one section that is tilting toward the ground at an alarming angle, and most do not have indoor plumbing. Public hand pumps stand at curbside, each one surrounded by a circle of ice. The townsfolk do not seem to appreciate these traditional houses, mostly populated by immigrants. The bulldozers are razing them and building high rise apartment buildings. When a wooden house burns in a fire, the chair of my department, Irina Fyodorovna, says,"I hope they all burn down."

But the Volkonsky House, now a museum, is quite an elegant wooden structure with high ceilings and a grand dining room. It was the home of Count Sergei Volkonsky, one of the Decembrist revolutionaries exiled to Siberia after trying to topple the czar in 1825. These nobles, and especially their wives, were largely responsible for making Irkutsk into an intellectual outpost.

The docent carefully follows me from room to room. I am the only visitor to the museum. In a quiet proud voice, she explains each portrait, each framed letter, the German piano, the desk transported by wagon from St. Petersburg. I imagine the effort on the part of those nobles to recreate the lives they had left in European Russia. Since I know how much work it is to keep our own wood stove going all winter, I am especially interested in the enormous tiled stoves throughout the house, each one spanning two rooms and heating both. There must have been an army of servants to keep stoking the stoves during the Siberian winter. There is an atrium full of plants; an orange tree bears a single fruit. Apparently Count Volkonsky had a green thumb; they kept the atrium warm all winter for his plants. "*Next year,*" the docent says, "*we may try to grow a banana tree.*"

"*During Soviet times,*" she says, "*this house was turned into communal apartments.*" I wonder how many people were squeezed into these rooms. Did they hang sheets between the families who shared the dining room? Did they stoke the enormous wood stoves? Was there a scramble to live closer to the stove?

Back in my apartment, the key turns in the lock without a knock; the *dezhurnaya* and the *kommandant* enter unbidden, carrying blankets and sheets. "*You will have neighbors,*" the *dezhurnaya* says, "*on Sunday.*" She and I are on good terms by now. I've shown her my family pictures, and she has told me her story. She was an economist, but now she's a pensioner. She's working at the desk and cleaning the halls to finance her grandson's education at the university. But our good relationship apparently won't keep people from moving into my apartment.

I always knew this would be a possibility. The International Relations Office originally told me it was a group apartment, but I had the fantasy that, since the semester was well under way, the Dean for International Students would forget that I was alone in a four-bedroom apartment.

"*I'm happy by myself,*" I tell the *dezhurnaya*. "*I don't want neighbors.*"

"*Only for one week.*"

"How many people?"

"Six."

That will be seven of us with one kitchen, one bath, two bathroom sinks, and two WC compartments. That sounds crowded to me. I have been gradually spreading out in the apartment. Just yesterday I made the big commitment. I bought a toilet seat in the Chinese market. There weren't too many choices; they were all those spongy padded seats, either Winnie the Pooh with metal hardware or a pastel blue model with plastic screws and flowers on top. I went for aesthetics rather than quality; I couldn't stand the idea of sitting on Pooh Bear for the next several months. I haven't yet had time to install the seat, so it is sitting in my closet.

"Should I move all my kitchen supplies into my room?" I ask the *dezhurnaya*. She peers into the cabinet where I keep onions, oatmeal, nuts and dried fruit, tea and spices. On the counter are the American water filter and the sprouter.

"You just tell them 'This is my cabinet,'" she says, *"and I will explain that a foreign teacher is living here for the semester. They won't cook here. They'll just use the electric kettle to make tea."*

I concentrate my kitchen supplies in one cabinet, stock the kitchen with fresh dish soap and a new sponge and the WC with toilet paper. In preparation for sharing the bathroom, I wash my laundry, so my clothesline that stretches across the washroom won't be full of drying clothes when other people need to wash up. I line the trash baskets with plastic bags and leave the kitchen equipment I purchased available for all to use: the forks and spoons, the bread knife, cutting board, grater, and dish drainer. But the new toilet seat remains in my closet.

On Sunday afternoon, when I return from the market, three large middle-aged women are sitting in my kitchen.

"Hello," I say. "My name is Vivian."

They are Irina, Natalya, and Olga, all schoolteachers from a Siberian city eight hours away, attending a seminar here in Irkutsk. None of them speaks English. A red-faced, burly man walks in the door carrying suitcases. "Viktor," he says when I introduce myself to him. Viktor and one of the women take the bedroom I rejected because it was too cold. I know that the refrigerator and TV still don't work, and the closet door is off its hinges. The other two women share a bedroom across the hall. Two more schoolteachers are due soon; they'll stay in the remaining bedroom.

I sit in my room with the door closed. They leave their doors open, calling loudly to each other from room to room. The two other women arrive. Then more people come in. I don't know who these people are. They all sit around the kitchen table. When I go into the kitchen to warm up some soup, they all rise and leave the kitchen to me. I take the pot of hot soup, a bowl, and spoon and bring them into my room to eat supper on the little table with my soap opera, *One Night of Love.*

The teachers bring in an enormous thermos, eggs, potatoes, jars of homemade pickles and jam, bread, butter, cookies. The first night they boil potatoes and eat them with pickles. They leave the leftovers in a pot against the window to keep cool.

When I go to wash up at night, Viktor is in the washroom smoking. Although he has opened the window, the odor of smoke drifts through the apartment.

"You shouldn't smoke," I say.

"Why?"

I don't want to start things off badly. "It's bad for your health," I say. Viktor looks like a man who drinks too much vodka and eats too much *sala*, the raw pig's lard.

"Also, it's forbidden to smoke in the dorm."

He doesn't respond, just keeps on smoking.

That night they sleep with their doors open to the hall while I sleep with my door closed and locked. There's no sight of anyone in the morning, just the hacking smoker's cough from the bedroom, again and again and again.

"I now have neighbors in my apartment," I tell my English class. We are comparing Russian and American attitudes toward the law. "They are smoking in the dorm. Do you think I should tell the *dezhurnaya*? They might feel they are back in the old Soviet days when neighbors reported on each other."

Tall slender Oleg has been consistently quiet in class, but he's a smoker, so he feels strongly about this. "You mustn't tell the *dezhurnaya*," he says. "It's a free country. I can smoke anywhere I want."

"Are you free to hurt someone else?"

That day I leave the university early so I can bathe and cook while there is no one in the apartment. I prepare a salad to eat with bread and cheese in my room. At night the teachers cook pasta and meat cutlets. They sit together in the kitchen eating and talking all evening. I huddle in my room with the door closed.

On Tuesday afternoon I again come home early to have the apartment to myself. The door to one of the toilets is locked. At first I assume that it's occupied, but after a long time, I realize that someone turned the knob so that it locked automatically when it was closed. It is the kind of knob we often have in bathrooms in the US, and I also have it on my bedroom here in Irkutsk; the center of the knob turned to horizontal locks behind you when you leave.

Three teachers come home from work and gather in the kitchen to prepare dinner.

"Did you cook today?" Olga asks me. She has a large pot of potatoes peeled and covered with water.

"No, I just made a salad."

"Because the stove isn't working."

Great. We are entering breakdown mode. I show them that one toilet is also out of commission because it is locked from within.

Viktor goes down to get the *kommandant*, but she is gone for the night. *"The dezhurnaya says they will fix the stove at nine o'clock tomorrow morning."*

Meanwhile, I remember I have a file on my Swiss army knife, so I go to work on the locked toilet. I insert the tip of the file in the slit in the doorknob. The ladies and Viktor watch in amazement as I manage to twist the knob until it opens.

"I'm a good thief," I say, and we all laugh. *"But please explain to the other ladies that they mustn't lock the door from the inside."*

On Wednesday when I get home to bathe and cook before the crowds arrive, no one has come to fix the stove. The raw potatoes are still soaking in the pot of water. The kitchen is starting to get messy. There's an open bowl of sugar. A fly is buzzing around cookies on a plate. The butter was left out, and so was the mayonnaise. There are cups with used tea bags next to an open box of tea. A large microwave has appeared on the table.

This time, it's the bathing compartment that is locked from the inside. Again I jimmy the latch. When everyone gets home, I conduct a lesson on the mechanics of the locks. Seven of us pile into the washroom. They chatter away as I show them the locked position and then the open position. For the finale, I duplicate the situation with the locked door. *"No, no!"* they shout. *"Don't lock it!*" Everyone tries unsuccessfully to open the door, and then I show them how I jimmy the lock.

"*When I'm tired of teaching,*" I say, "*I will have a new profession.*"

"*A thief,*" they say.

Everyone has sandwiches for supper, I in my room with my soap opera, they in the kitchen. I check my bedroom lock to see if it's as easy to jimmy as the bathroom and toilet, but fortunately it isn't.

On Thursday morning, on my way out of the dorm, I knock on the *kommandant's* door.

"*The stoves on all the floors in that line aren't working,*" she says as if the situation is hopeless.

"*Then it must be the electricity in that line,*" I say.

"*I have tried to get someone to come, but they don't respond.*"

"*We are seven people in that apartment, and we need a stove,*" I say as forcefully as I can.

In my Russian grammar class, my situation sparks a discussion about dorm rooms. In the student apartments, sixteen students live in a space the size of my apartment, four in each bedroom. The foreign students, all Chinese, think I am living in great luxury in my current condition.

After class I go to the Dean's office. "*We are seven people in the apartment. This is the third day with no stove,*" I say.

In Russia always go directly to the top. By the time I get home, the stove is functioning. When my neighbors hear that I reported it to the Dean, I am the hero of the apartment. They can finally cook their potatoes.

During a commercial in my soap opera, I go to the kitchen to get a spoon. Four ladies and Viktor are sitting around the table that is set with platters of sliced fish, meat and cheese, potatoes, fried eggs, and pickles. A bottle of vodka is on the table. It's their farewell dinner.

"*Priyatnovo appetita,*" I say, using the traditional words when interrupting people eating.

"*Vivian,*" Olga says, "*come join us. This is our last night, and you are the one who got the stove fixed and unlocked the doors. Do you drink vodka?*"

My soap opera isn't finished, and I have already eaten, but I sit down with them. They teach in a rural school. Olga is the principal. Natalya and Irina are teachers of Russian language. Lidia teaches math. Their school was selected for this conference because of its excellent record. Viktor is the driver.

"*We are from the village,*" they say. They are proud of their homemade pickles just as I am.

"*Have you ever had a homegrown egg?*" Lidia asks.

"*Are these your eggs?*"

"*No, they are the chicken's.*" Everyone laughs. She wants me to eat the egg raw with vodka, but I tell her I'll have it for breakfast in the morning. I also try to be polite as I refuse the *sala,* the raw pork fat Russians insist is a healthy companion to vodka.

"*I am from the village too,*" I say. I show them the pictures of my home and fields in Massachusetts, Chapel Brook behind our house, Frank in muck boots, standing on a bale of mulch hay, holding a hoe.

"*Gladioli,*" they say, pointing, "*and lettuce and onions.*"

"*Do you grow bananas?*" Viktor asks.

"*No, Viktor,*" Natalya says. "*It's the North, just like it is here.*"

"*Well, not quite as cold,*" I say. Siberians love to hear that it is colder here than anywhere else. It's a matter of pride that they can

106

tolerate more cold than anyone. With my hand I measure how high the snow is in Massachusetts.

More vodka, more toasts, and then some fire water they call homemade *visky*. They write down the recipe for me. Natalya recites passages from *Eugene Onegin*. Then comes the singing. I'm ready for some sweet harmony such as I have heard in Ukraine, but these ladies wail it out, slightly flat, yet strong and confident. Sometimes Viktor joins in, and sometimes he cries at the words of the songs. They present me with a notebook from their conference. I give them stickers for their students that say "Great!" and "Awesome!" in English. We take pictures; we exchange addresses. Eventually we stagger off to bed.

In the morning they scrub the kitchen and use the rag to wash all the floors in the apartment. When they are packed and ready to go, they knock on my door. One by one the ladies kiss me goodbye. Viktor is already downstairs with the car. And so I learn something about communal living in Russia.

When the apartment is quiet once more, I use the plastic screws to attach the spongy blue toilet seat with white flowers.

Angara River, Irkutsk, Siberia. 2008

Bad Student

The Chinese students in my Russian as a Second Language class have adopted Russian names. Tanya, with brittle hair in a ponytail, knows her grammar. She always corrects the rest of us when we speak. Pretty Irina joined the class after I did. She says that she had to return to China because she was ill, but now she's back. She's often late to class and rarely has done her homework. Misha is a poet. He sits in the front row and answers very seriously. Bespectacled Anton often sits next to me. He says that English was his first foreign language, but now he feels his Russian is stronger. We never speak English together, though. Wei-wei, who doesn't seem to have a Russian name, is the other person I sometimes sit with. She shares her pronunciation pages with me and always answers our instructor, Tamara Nikolaevna, by reading verbatim from the text. Then there is Vanya. He stumbles in with sleepy eyes half an hour late every morning. Every day the teacher asks why he is late, and he says he is sick, but when he isn't in class, she says, *"Vanya is not a serious person."* Vanya is in charge of making copies of the teacher's book for all the other students. We pay a ruble a page.

There's another student in the class, a gray-haired American English teacher who enjoys reciting the poems and songs. Tamara Nikolaevna says this student speaks like she is from the Volga, pronouncing all the unaccented *o*'s *oh* instead of *ah*. She always does her homework but hates taking the tests. She is the only one in the class that ever says, *"I don't understand,"* or *"Where are we on the page?"* or *"What does that word mean?"* Am I the only one who is ever confused?

Tamara Nikolaevna is lively and good-natured, but she mostly uses the reading as a source of vocabulary development. Even when I supply the chalk, she doesn't use the blackboard although it would be very helpful. Occasionally she asks us to write factual questions about the text for the other students to answer. Which composers did the author mention? Where did he grow up? At the moment we are reading about personality characteristics and professions.

"*Are you rude or polite?*" she asks Tanya.

"*I'm polite.*" It's true; all these Chinese young people are polite.

"*Are you brave or cowardly?*" she asks Wei-wei.

"*I'm brave.*" Also true. They are all quite brave to come to Russia to study.

"*Who is talented in the class?*" she asks Misha.

"*Vivian, because she is a writer.*"

"*I don't feel talented,*" I say. "*I feel incompetent because I can't remember anything in Russian.*"

I really have the best intentions, but I am not a model student. There's a temptation to say it's not my fault—I have other responsibilities here—but that's what all my students at home would say too. No matter what the excuse, the fact is a student learns or doesn't learn. I always say this at Holyoke Community College in Massachusetts, and now it is coming back to haunt me.

When I first started auditing the class, nearly two months ago in the middle of their academic year, I didn't know how Irina Nikolaevna could understand these students from China; to me their Russian sounded just like Chinese. This must be how my ESL students feel when they try to understand each other in my class at Holyoke Community College. At the end of my first class, the instructor asked Misha to show me where I could make copies of the text for the homework.

On the way to the copy center, I asked him how long he had been in Irkutsk.

"I'm sorry," he said. *"I don't speak English."*

"But," I said, *"I am speaking Russian."*

Now when my fellow students speak, I understand them much better. It's possible their Russian pronunciation has greatly improved with the benefit of fourteen hours of Russian study per week. Or else I have gotten accustomed to their Chinese accents. They also seem to understand me better even though I only attend seven hours per week.

Our etiquette class hasn't met for three weeks, but supposedly, when it does, we will have a test on accepting and declining invitations. Half the time the Russian grammar class conflicts with the English classes I teach, so I never know the grammar homework, and I never have copies of the pages.

Every so often my role as visiting English professor interferes even more with my Russian classes, but I try to avoid this. The Chair of American Studies wants to change the scheduled time of the biweekly seminar that I offer the American Studies teachers.

"I'm not free at that time. I have Russian."

"Then you can miss it that day."

"Russian is very important to me," I say. "I don't want to miss it."

My Russian grammar teacher, Valentina Olegovna, announces a grammar test on verbal prefixes on the morning I will be returning to Irkutsk by train after visiting a nearby city Ulan Ude. I tell her that I don't think I will take the test.

"Why not?"

"Well, I miss half the classes, and I don't have any books." Those seem like good reasons to me. I don't yet have a sense of what these verbal prefixes mean. In my dictionary, *za-* as a prefix can

mean "the start of an action," as in "I started to talk." Or it can mean "en route," such as "We talked en route to the store." Or it can mean "to the point of forgetfulness," such as "We were talking so much on the trolley that we forget to get off." Those seem like totally different meanings to me. Some of the prefixes have six different meanings.

"You should take the test anyway," Valentina Olegovna says. *"It's good for you."* And she lends me the books for my trip.

I have been away for three days without much time to study. On the train I try to study from the textbook my teacher lent me, but it is so ancient and obtuse, and the copy is so poorly printed that I nod off every time I open the book. I agonize about whether to present myself at the university to take the test. My own students at Holyoke Community College and university students here in Irkutsk don't show up when they aren't prepared. That seems like a good idea to me at this moment. However, I have to return Valentina Olegovna's books, so I guess I'll have to take the test and make an idiot of myself.

When I get to the university the morning of the test, the class is not in any of the rooms where it has met before; I go to the Dean's office. My other Russian teacher, Tamara Nikolaevna, is sitting at a desk in the office.

"Good morning," I say. *"I've just arrived from Ulan Ude. Where's the grammar class?"*

"They're having a test," she says.

"I know."

I must look pretty glum because Tamara Nikolaevna says, *"Valentina Olegovna isn't here. She's sick. Do you want to take the test?"*

I shake my head.

"Well, then, don't take it. Go home and have a rest." In Massa-

114

chusetts, I once had a student whom I told to skip the tests. They made him very nervous, and he was hopeless anyway. Maybe it's the same for me.

I miss Valentina Olegovna's grammar class all week since my English classes have been rescheduled due to a holiday. Now they completely conflict with my Russian classes. But one morning I see Valentina Olegovna in the hall. Maybe she is wondering what happened to my test paper or why I haven't been in class. I slink past her without speaking just as my own ESL students would do.

I can't turn my phone off in Russian class because I don't know where I will teach next. Someone must call me to tell me the room number. I finally have learned how to mute my phone, but before I figured it out, I received several calls in the middle of class, including one from my daughter Tobey in Oregon. Today Tamara Nikolaevna answers a call in class, and several students' phones ring with messages, but at least that doesn't happen to me any more.

Our Russian class has a project we will present to a panel of faculty soon; we don't know exactly when. Tamara Nikolaevna originally said we could choose any topic; she gave as an example that we could study the churches of Irkutsk. Since no one seemed to have any other ideas, that became our topic. Each student will talk about one church. We will also create a calendar of our photographs of the churches. The calendar will be mounted on a large wooden cross. By American standards, it seems like a strangely sectarian topic for students of a public university; I wonder what all these young Chinese students, probably Communists in good standing, definitely not Christians, think of this project.

When Tamara Nikolaevna is talking about the churches, I ask, *"Is there a synagogue in Irkutsk?"*

She looks at me for a moment. I know the answer to the question; I'm just causing trouble.

"*I don't know,*" she says. "*There is a mosque somewhere.*"

One day when I was walking about town, I saw the roof of an ornate old building with a Star of David carved on the top. The building was not easy to find from the ground, but when I did, it had a sign that said it was a bureau for workers. Maybe it had been an old synagogue. Later I read that there is a functioning synagogue somewhere in Irkutsk, but I haven't found it yet.

The church Tamara Nikolaevna assigns me no longer exists. It was the enormous Kazansky Cathedral that dominated the main square of Irkutsk, the same square where the university stands now. The cathedral was 200 feet high and so massive that its footprint came all the way to what is now the central fountain. It was the defining structure of Irkutsk. In 1932 it was blown up, around the same time all the Buddhist temples were destroyed. The literature uses the passive voice. Who blew up the cathedral? No one is taking responsibility now. In its place was constructed the ugly regional administration building. All that remains in memory of the cathedral is a small cupola in front of this white government building. Through the cupola's locked gate, a mournful Madonna and Child stare out. Now there is a movement to tear down the Soviet administration building and reconstruct the cathedral. This is human history, the pyramids in Mexico, the Buddhas of Bamiyan, the Temple Mount in Jerusalem. It's not enough to conquer a culture. It's necessary to annihilate its holy spots.

The story of this cathedral sparks my imagination, but I don't like the prospect of giving an oral report in Russian to a panel of judges. The other students seem to be memorizing their presentations. Misha will give the introduction, and he has memorized about three pages, including a postscript that Tamara Nikolaevna added about the existence of a synagogue and mosque in Irkutsk. If Misha loses his place in his recitation, I'm afraid he will have to go back to the beginning and start again. I won't try to memorize the story of Kazansky Cathedral. I'll use my miniscule vocabulary and incorrect grammar, but at least I'll know what I am speaking about.

The day that we construct the calendar of churches, the Chinese students and I spend many hours with tape and scissors.

"*How do you like studying in Irkutsk?*" I ask them.

"*It's boring,*" Wei-wei says. I'm not surprised to hear her say this. Every time they report what they did the day before, they always say, "*I did my homework*" or "*I cooked dinner.*" I think they spend a lot of time in their rooms.

"*Irkutsk is too expensive,*" Misha says. "*The dorms are lousy.*"

"*We miss our parents,*" Tanya says.

"*What about you?*" I ask Irina. "*You went to China, and then you returned to Irkutsk.*" Irina seems to have a boyfriend in another class. I've seen them holding hands in the hall.

"*I don't want to be here,*" she says. "*I want to go home.*"

"*For me it's interesting in Irkutsk,*" I say.

"*We're too young to be away from home,*" Wei-wei says.

There are about two hundred foreign students at different levels of Russian study, most of them from China and Korea. They all live together in the dorm.

"*Every day,*" Anton says, "*I go to the central market. I like to cook.*"

"*So do I.*"

"*What do you cook?*" he asks.

"*Simple things: soup, omelets, salads, vegetables.*"

"*Vegetables are too expensive,*" he says.

Suddenly I have an idea. How do you say "tofu" in Russian?

Soon I am on my way. The Chinese market is on Sofi Perovskoi Street; everyone calls that block *Shanghaiska*. The students described a Chinese grocery, but there are several stores with Chinese signs. The first one I walk into sells construction supplies. The second sells food, but the owner directs me to another store on the corner. In a plastic vat to the right of the door are enormous fluffy squares of *dofu*, soaking in water. When the storekeeper puts two squares in a plastic bag for me, they are still warm, freshly pressed.

He is amazed to see me. *"Where are you from? Do they have dofu in America? It's the Chinese people who make it, right?"*

I don't try to tell him how much tofu I have consumed in my life, that my husband used to be called Tofu Frank and worked in one of the first American tofu factories, that we have made tofu lasagna, tofu sloppy Joes, scrambled tofu, tofu icing, tofu pudding, tofu steaks, that now in the US people eat tofurkey and tofu hotdogs. It is enough to have my new treasure to carry home in a leaking plastic bag.

In the morning, when Tamara Nickolaevna asks us for the daily report, I say, *"I bought tofu in the market."*

She taught in China for two years. *"Really? Where?"*

"How did you cook it?" Misha asks. Everyone in class turns to look at me.

I made soup and stir-fry and fried tofu. I used garlic and oil and soy sauce. I cooked buckwheat groats and Chinese cabbage, scallions, and peppers. I have eaten a kilo of tofu since yesterday.

After class Tamara Nikolaevna rushes off to *Shanghaiska*.

Ice fishing, Irkutsk, Siberia. 2008

Siberian Village

The phone wakes me at midnight as I am fading into sleep. I expect it to be my family calling from twelve or fifteen time zones away. But it is Alex, the young botanist whom I met in Ulan Ude when we both slept on the living room floor of a young Fulbright researcher. Alex and I have met here in Irkutsk since then to practice English and Russian together. Now on the phone Alex is speaking in English, of a sort.

"Vivian, you like Baikal?"

"Baikal is wonderful." I scramble to turn on a light. Maybe this is an appropriate hour for Russian phone calls.

"We are seeing Baikal. It's very beautiful for you. OK?"

"What, Alex?"

" *Murino* at Baikal, very good place. Good for you." He mentions something else, *Katanka* or *Tarzhanka* or some such. I guess that's a village.

"When?" I ask.

"How do you say *subbotu?*"

"Saturday."

"I see you train station nine o'clock morning. OK?"

There are four different entrances to the central train station, and I didn't get the name of the place he wants to go.

"You are free? How do you say *subbotu?*"

"Saturday. Yes, I'm free. I don't have classes on Friday either."

"No? Good. Then we meet at five o'clock."

"Five in the morning?"

"No!" He sounds alarmed.

"OK, Alex. 5 PM Friday? Or Saturday?" It must be an overnight trip. "Where will we sleep?"

"One person's house, my old friend. To him sixty, very old. He tells house is free. I buy my Notebook, my dream, with Skype. For 4,250 rubles. Bring DVDs. I see you my office two o'clock. Internet."

I'm not getting this. "When will we return to Irkutsk?"

"Tuesday. How do you say *voskryeshenye?*"

"Sunday."

"How do you say *pyatnitsa?*"

"Friday. Alex, which *marshrutka* goes to your office?"

"I call you tomorrow."

That's probably what I sound like in Russian. From this conversation, I have no idea when, where, what, or with whom. Am I ready for another weekend in very close quarters with Alex?

I discuss this phone call with the English teachers in the American Studies office. No one is familiar with any villages called Murino or Katanka or Tarzhanka, but Olga says that if I have the opportunity to go to a village on Baikal, I should go.

"He called me at midnight. He mentioned Friday, Tuesday, Saturday, Sunday. It was very confusing."

"Was he sober?" Dariya asks.

The next evening I call him first, so that he won't wake me at midnight again. I tell him to speak to me in Russian. At least that way one of us will know what is being said. It seems he is inviting me to go to a village named Murino on the south end of Lake Baikal near the town of Baikalsk. We will leave on Friday evening. My understanding is that there will be another man, a friend of Alex's, who I think is also some kind of scientist. This

124

person has access to a big house, and we can stay there for the weekend, returning on Sunday. Alex wants me to meet him at his office at the botanical gardens at Irkutsk State University. He tells me the *marshrutka* to take to get to his work and says I should call him when I arrive at the bus stop.

I picture a camp of some sort in the snowy woods with some white-bearded Russian scientist. I don't know Alex very well, and I feel apprehensive, but if I want to see anything besides the route between my dormitory and the university, I might as well accept opportunities when they arise.

"*I bought a Notebook,*" he says.

"*That part I understood. Congratulations. Is there internet at this house in Murino?*"

"*Not at all!*" Of course not. What a ridiculous American question! There probably isn't even running water, but Alex keeps making some connection I don't understand between the new laptop and Murino.

"*Will there be a lot of snow there?*" I ask. "*And should I buy food?*" Winter camping probably requires carrying in all the supplies we need.

"*As you like. It's not necessary. I am buying meat.*" That sounds like *shashlik*, the ubiquitous Russian shish kabob. How do I prepare for this trip?

I buy bread, cheese, ham, and fruit. At least we will have something to eat on the train. Alex carries a flask of vodka and two plastic bags of meat he is marinating for *shashlik*. It's a good thing we didn't meet at the train station, because he was referring to a different station, one for the *elektrichka*, a sort of commuter train that passes right by Alex's place of work at the botanical gardens.

"We will get on the second to the last car," he says. We have switched mostly to Russian.

When we embark, sitting in the seat by the door is an attractive middle-aged woman holding the leash of an enormous white Samoyed. We sit opposite her.

"This is my friend Nadia," Alex says. *"And this . . .,"* pointing to the dog, *". . . is Archie."*

At first I think it is a coincidence that we met Nadia on the train, but gradually I realize that she and Archie are accompanying us to Murino. For me, that's a reassuring sign. I am not going to outer space alone with a twenty-eight-year-old expert on Russian ferns. The train trip takes four hours. Now I understand the purpose of the laptop. It is a traveling entertainment center. Alex puts in a pirated DVD, five movies on one disk. Nadia joins us on our bench, and Archie, who has his own train ticket, climbs onto her seat. Tony Curtis and Jack Lemmon in drag, speaking with the same Russian voice isn't bad, but Marilyn Monroe with a male voice in Russian is surrealistic. We watch the movie, and Archie watches us.

I wonder if the sight of Lake Baikal will continue to amaze me each time I see it. It is beyond fathoming, iced over for fifty miles across and five hundred miles to the north. It seems impossible, the epitome of Siberia, so stark, so endless. At first, I was intrigued by the Siberian custom of traveling on the ice in the winter by car, along or across the lake, until one of the teachers at the university told me that sixteen cars had sunk to the bottom of Baikal this winter.

"What about the people in the cars?"

"They sank too. This happens every year."

Too horrible to contemplate. The lake is both enchanting and terrifying.

Alex's plan is actually very civilized. Murino isn't the wilderness even if it is remote. It's an inhabited village. When we disembark, a kind-faced man named Yura is waiting for us with a small pickup truck. We pile all our bags in the back, and I, as the foreign guest, am seated in the front. Alex, Nadia, and Archie walk while Yura drives five minutes to a single-story house in a fenced yard. I am whisked through two layers of doors and behind a woolen blanket blocking the draft into a cozy kitchen heated by a brick woodstove. Yura's large and powerful wife, Anna, arrives right after Alex and Nadia. I am in the bosom of the family, welcomed with tea and a hot meal, supplied with slippers and a seat by the stove. There are fresh eggs, cow's milk, homemade pickles and marinated tomatoes, and an ample supply of firewood. There is a room for Nadia and me to share. Alex has his own spot. The only inconvenience is the toilet out in the backyard, a two-squatter down a winding path in the knee-high snow.

In the morning Lake Baikal is enshrouded in mist, disappearing into forever. Huge waves of ice rise up at the shore as if frozen in the moment before they could come crashing down. Time seems at a standstill. We step onto the lake past the waves that never arrived. The only sound is our feet squeaking on the snow. Below us the water is nearly a mile deep.

Lake Baikal is both everchanging and always the same, a massive expanse of silence. Each time I approach the lake, the chill air suddenly fills me with dread and anticipation.

Later in the bright afternoon sun, the distant shore, fifty miles away, is clearly discernible. In the middle mysterious forms seem to hover. We walk again onto the lake in single file, farther and farther from the security of the shore. Where are we going? The lake draws us and then engulfs us. We are silent in its silence.

I am walking ahead of the others. Suddenly, instead of holding my weight , the crust of the snow starts to break with each footprint. Compared to the depth of the water, the ice that sustains me seems terrifyingly fragile.

"*Come back, Vivian,*" Nadia says. "*It's water.*"

Terrified, I race back toward the land. But, of course, the ice is a meter thick; even if the very top is starting to melt. I won't sink into Baikal and be lost forever.

The bottomless lake is the epitome of the deep love these Siberians have for the land. Alex maintains two greenhouses and a large plot for rare indigeneous plants. Anna is a forest ranger. Nadia is a landscape gardener, and Yura a retired fisherman.

"*I was born here,*" Yura says. "*And I'll die here.*"

And then there is Archie, the great Siberian dog who sleeps in an unheated storage room all winter long. He silently suffered through the heat of the train to get to his beloved woods and snow.

We spend the days walking, walking. Down the road toward the mountains and then into the *taiga*, the Siberian forest. We come to a steep embankment. Below is a frozen river. In the spring the waters will flow into Baikal. Families are building fires on the snow for Siberian picnics. A cable is suspended across the river with a swing hanging from it. The local people, adults as well as children, shriek with excitement as they hurtle across the river. This is the *tarzanka*, named for Tarzan, that Alex had tried to describe in his midnight call. And next to it is the *katanye*, a steep sledding hill that ends in the river.

"*You must try it,*" Alex says to me after he has whizzed down the hill on a plastic bag. "*You have to try everything.*"

I don't like the looks of the *katanye*; it appears to be very icy. Physical daring isn't my strong suit. I prefer snowshoes to downhill skiing. I like flat ice, not precipices. But my hosts are eagerly awaiting my initiation; this is their offering to the foreign visitor. To refuse would be to reject their hospitality. Alex asks for my camera to document the event. My timidity on the slide probably disappoints him; I take it as slowly as I can, but for some reason the *tarzanka* doesn't inspire the same fear in me. All the neighbors stop their activities to see what will happen as I climb onto the swinging seat. I push off and go screaming across the frozen river as exhilarated as a ten-year-old, crashing into the snowdrift on the opposite shore.

A young boy runs down the stairs to the river to help me drag the swing back by its long rope.

"Do you know New York?" he asks shyly.

Talking to this strange American lady in the red stocking cap seems more amazing to him than flying through the air above a frozen river in Siberia.

Eating is the other great entertainment. I think we eat five meals a day. There is breakfast and then *chai*, not just tea, but an entire new meal with bread and cheese, pickles, preserves, fruit, and whatever is left over from breakfast. Then there is lunch and then *chai* again in the mid-afternoon. Next comes dinner, lasting for hours and including multiple toasts of vodka and homemade *visky*. The men are in charge of the cooking on the brick wood stove or on a two-burner hotplate, but the premium cooking location is the outdoor sheet metal trough with its wood fire. There Alex concocts an enormous pot of *plov*, rice with dried wild mushrooms and large quantities of garlic. There he grills his succulent pork *shashlik*. Yura also takes his turn and grills whole fresh *omul*, fish from Lake Baikal.

Over these meals, we talk and talk. My Russian is improving by the hour. They speak of the conflicts between the longtime residents and the newcomers with their fancy recreational *dachas*. There is also the threat to Lake Baikal from the Soviet-era paper mill in Slyudyanka. When the wind turns, the putrid odor drifts all the way to Murino.

"People in Moscow don't care about us here," Alex says. *"Irkutsk region is very rich, but we don't get any of the profits. For the gas that comes from the North, they are building a pipeline too close to Baikal."*

"Did people work together better under Communism?"

"Communism was worse," Yura says. *"Everyone was always afraid."*

Nadia offers a toast to Alex, who has provided us with the delicious meals.

The talk turns to grizzly bears, wolves, wild boars, and Baikal's *nerpa* seals, the only freshwater seals in the world. Yura talks about his domestic turkeys, chickens, and rabbits. I tell them about porcupines, skunks, and deer in Massachusetts.

Yura toasts to me, the guest who has come such a long way.

We compare our gardens. They have ninety-seven frost-free days and haven't had any luck growing Brussels sprouts or fresh corn.

"You must see Baikal in the summer," Anna says. *"Everything is in bloom. We enjoy ourselves so much."*

"You seem to enjoy the winter," I say. I cannot imagine Baikal as anything but a frozen expanse.

"Please come back with your husband in June," Yura says. *"I'll take him fishing on Lake Baikal, and we'll go into the mountains."*

I toast to my hosts who have opened their home and their hearts to me.

Alex toasts to friendship across continents, across cultures. We empty our shot glasses.

"*So, what is the nature of God?*" Yura begins.

Irkutsk lady, Siberia. 2008

Agreeing and Disagreeing

My Russian etiquette teacher has been absent nearly a month; no one has replaced her, and no one has even notified us that there won't be a class. Each class meeting the Chinese students and I sit outside the locked classroom waiting for Liza to arrive, but no one ever comes. This is actually not a great loss since her teaching method isn't inspiring; we simply read lists of expressions about agreeing and disagreeing.

Anton reads, "*No. Of course not. Most definitely not. Absolutely not. In no way. I can't agree. I don't agree.*"

Valentina: "*It's impossible to agree. On the contrary. I absolutely and completely disagree.*"

Tanya: "*Incorrect. Certainly not. Impossible.*"

"*Maybe Liza will come today,*" I say to Misha as we wait for her on the fourth week. "*But if she does, I hope she won't give us the test after all this time.*"

"*She won't,*" he says.

It wouldn't be very good etiquette or very good pedagogy. We have a new student in our class, a Korean whose name sounds like Jowang. He seems totally lost, but I felt that way too when I first arrived. Jowang's English is clearly better than his Russian. He would like me to translate for him from Russian into English, but mostly I don't do it. I don't want to speak English in Russian class, and he also needs to try to understand the Russian.

This week Liza finally comes to class. She asks the new student his name, writes it down in her book, and proceeds to dictate a test to us. Jowang is quite upset since he doesn't understand her instructions and because this is his first time in etiquette class. Of course, he doesn't know the material.

After the test, Liza says, *"This is my last class with you. I am leaving the university. I'm going to have a baby."*

"Congratulations," I say. *"Who will teach us etiquette?"*

"I don't know," she says.

As we are reading interminable ways to express regret, the loud speaker announces that there is a small fire somewhere at the university.

"What shall we do?" Liza asks the class.

"Go home," says Wei-Wei.

In the hall students from other rooms are milling around. They return to their classrooms, but we depart for the day, and that is the last we see of Liza.

What a shame. I am deeply sorry. I can't tell you how sorry I am. How unfortunate. Too bad.

The first year English translation students are working on their pronunciation, in particular "the American variant," as they say in the American Studies Department. I had an argument with Alex the botanist about British and American English.

"Different languages," he said. "I get two (a grade of D) British English and five (an A) American English. So they not one language."

Flawless logic. I wonder what the teacher of American English was thinking when she gave him a five.

I often use poetry to teach pronunciation. It's especially useful for practicing the rhythm of the language. The students love working with poetry, but the teacher I am mentoring isn't interested. She rustles her papers, rips them up into pieces and makes such a racket that finally I say to her, "What are you doing, Svetlana Nikolaevna?"

After more rustling, she leaves the classroom and doesn't return for fifteen minutes. I guess she feels there is nothing she can learn from observing me and that I am working with her class to give her time to organize her papers.

The students and I discuss the fact that Robert Frost may not be talking literally about the Apocalypse when he says the world may end in fire or in ice.

"In your opinion, which is stronger, desire or hate?" I ask. But, given that this is Siberia, I can't resist adding, "So, do you think the world will end in fire or ice?"

"Ice," they say.

People in Irkutsk tell me the winters are not as severe here as they were in the past, that the ice on Lake Baikal doesn't get solid until later in the year. Russia is doing more drilling for oil and gas in the Arctic because the polar ice caps are melting.

I write "Global warming" on the board. "Do you know this expression?" I ask.

"Some people believe the earth is warming," Lara says, "but some believe it is getting colder."

"Which people are those?"

Usually Lara is very smart. "An equal number of scientists believe that we are entering a new cold period."

I am reading about Russian denial on a massive scale in *The Gulag Archipelago*. Global warming is just an opinion, the way evolution is an opinion, the way the existence of the Holocaust is an opinion. Believe what you want to believe.

This attitude comes up again in an English Speaking and Listening class. We are talking about food and culture. I write American idioms for food on the board: takeout, potluck, wolf down, pig out, eat out, all you can eat. Junk food is one expression they know.

"So, what is junk food?" I ask.

Like many Americans, the Russians love fat and sugar. Skim milk doesn't exist here. Sour cream is a daily staple, and so is raw lard, *sala*. Sausages, kielbasa, large slatherings of mayonnaise. The meat of choice is pork. The average life expectancy for a Russian man is about fifty-eight and declining.

"Chips are junk food," says Galya.

"Right."

"Soft drinks," Larisa, the teacher, chimes it.

"Definitely."

"Hamburgers," says Dasha. They like to think that Americans eat nothing but junk food.

"Don't forget candy," I say.

"Candy isn't junk food," Ella says. The ads on TV advertise milk chocolate as a nutritious source of milk for children.

"Chocolate has lots of vitamins in it," the teacher says.

"Russian chocolate isn't junk food," Dariya says. "But Snickers, that's junk food."

"Chocolate can't be junk food," Ella repeats, "because it's too delicious."

In an American Studies Speaking and Listening class, we have been talking politics. I discuss with them some differences between the Democratic and Republican parties. They have read about the legislative process, but the young teacher Olga\ says they didn't do well on their test. To make it more meaningful for the students, I present them with a problem to solve. I divide the class into four Democrats and four Republicans. Olga will be the Republican president.

There is a lake bordering both California and Nevada. The lake is considered a national heritage site, but there is an old paper factory that is polluting the lake. Environmentalists and local citizens have asked their Democratic congressman to present a bill to solve this problem. Artyom will represent the district in the House of Representatives.

The Democrats caucus, as do the Republicans. The Democrats decide to present a bill to clean up the lake with federal funds and federal regulations. In their caucus, Republicans don't want a federal bill at all. They decide to propose that the industry regulate itself. Then the legislators go to their respective Houses. Democrats in the Senate and the House present their bills.

"And where will the money come from to pay for this?" I ask.

"We are Democrats," Anya says in the House. "We are not adverse to raising taxes if necessary."

"And whom will you tax?" I ask.

"Tax the rich," German, a Democratic senator, calls from the other side of the room.

"No," Republican Senator Nadia says. "This is America. Everyone is equal. Everyone needs to pay taxes equally."

"Anyway, we Republicans are opposed to raising taxes," Denis says.

The students' first reaction is gridlock.

"Remember," I say, "in the US, the House Democrats have a majority. If you stick together, you can pass a bill that the Republicans object to. You Senate Democrats need to compromise more because the Republicans can filibuster and talk about their grandmothers forever."

Nadia, the esteemed senator from the state of Washington, nods her head as if that's just what she plans to do.

"But everyone needs to remember," I say, "that there is a Republican president." I point to the teacher, petite, lovely Olga, sitting in the front of the room. She grins sheepishly. "And she has to pass the bill to make it law."

In the House, the Republicans object to the Federal money being spent on the cleanup project. They don't like the regulatory agency. Then Denis starts to get creative. He suggests that the Federal government give a subsidy to a new company that will create filters for the factory. The Democrats confer. Is this some kind of Republican trick? Artyom is in a dilemma because his district contains the environmentalists, the tourist business, the employees of the factory, and the owner. He likes the idea of a cleanup that will save the factory, and he's willing to spend the federal dollars on industry to do it. It looks like the House will pass the bill if the Republicans will agree to a very small tax increase and some government regulation.

In the Senate, the Republicans are stonewalling. They say the paper factory should raise the price of the paper and the tourist industry should raise the tourist prices in the area to pay for the clean up.

"Give the cost to the consumers," Nadia says.

The Senate is at an impasse. I think we are about to hear the story of Nadia's grandmother.

The Democrats groan. "Does it ever happen that no bill gets passed?" Anton asks.

"It happens all the time," I say. "By the way, where would this new filter factory be located?"

"Probably in China," someone says.

"What can you offer at least one Senate Republican so she will vote for the bill?" I ask. "What state do you represent, Nadia, Washington?"

The Democrats start to look at each other. "What if we use federal funds to locate the filter factory in Nadia's state?" Anton says. "More business in your state, Nadia. What do you say?"

The bill in the House is unanimous. In the Senate, Nadia votes in favor, and only Dasha is opposed.

The bell rings to mark the end of the period. Nobody gets up to leave.

"Let's see what the president decides," I say.

"Well," Olga says. "I think this bill is good for Republicans. It's good for business. There will be only minor industry regulation. I'll pass this bill."

And so what has happened? The Federal tax money will go to subsidize a business located in Washington State. The company will probably outsource its filter manufacturing to China, so no workers will benefit from the new company. The filters may or may not properly clean up the pollution of a lake located between California and Nevada.

"Is this a real lake?" Anya asks.

"Yes, there really is a lake between California and Nevada."

"Is this a real problem?" Anton asks.

"It's a real problem somewhere. Where is the problem?"

"Lake Baikal," Artyom says.

I try this exercise again when I "lecture" for Irina Fyodoro- vna while she has the flu. Mariya Vasileyvna, our senior English faculty member, has asked to observe the lecture. There are forty students in the class, with a very inattentive group of young men sitting in the back. I make them all get up and join Democratic or Republican caucuses. In this class the two parties have much less trouble coming to an agreement. This time, however, they face a recalcitrant president. Mariya Vasileyvna doesn't want to participate, but I declare she is the president and needs to make a decision about this bill.

"Your American president is very stupid," she says. "So I will veto this law."

"Well, that's the end of the bill," I say.

"No," says Alyona from the House. "We can override the veto with a two thirds majority." And they do just that, with a unanimous vote in the House and nearly unanimous in the Senate. Only in Russia. All the students, even the deadbeats from the back, walk out of the class, talking animatedly.

"A great class," Mariya Vasileyvna says, "very inspiring."

After the next period, I meet her again in the American Studies office. She is flushed with excitement. "In my graduate students' class," she says, "we continued to discuss *The Dead Poets' Society*." I led a discussion with her students about that movie a few days ago, at which time the students disagreed on who was responsible for Neil's suicide, the rigid father or the permissive teacher.

"I had each student take a role in the movie," Mariya says, "and speak for that character. One student took the part of Neil and spoke from the grave."

Who says you can't teach an old dog?

Desk and chairs, Elista, Russia. 2009

A Taste of Tajikistan

When I tell the teachers at the American Studies Department that I have an invitation from the US embassy in Tajikistan to give workshops to English teachers, they all shake their heads.

"It's dangerous there," Irina Fyodorovna says. "Civil war."

"But that ended eleven years ago."

"Aren't you afraid?" Larisa asks.

I need permission from the Fulbright Office in Moscow to work outside Russia during the period of my grant. "We don't recommend that people go to Tajikistan," the assistant at the office writes.

I have already read on the internet that last winter in Tajikistan was very severe with a record amount of snow that closed the route between the two main cities, Dushanbe and Khujand. Temperatures dipped to -30°C/-22°F, and homes in many parts of the country were without power or heat. During the winter there was an advisory, warning Americans from traveling to Tajikistan because of extreme weather conditions. But, by now, it is spring and the temperatures in Dushanbe are in the balmy seventies.

The embassy cultural attaché in Dushanbe assures me that Americans are favorably received, that the weather is great. She is very surprised by the reactions in Moscow. However, her official request yields clearance from the Fulbright director.

"Tajikistan is a very ugly country," a student says when I announce to my class I will be away from Irkutsk.

"I don't think so. It may be poor, but according to what I see on the internet, it is quite beautiful."

As soon as I board the plane, I am in a different country. There must be two dozen small children on this jet. Every Tajik woman on the plane seems to be nursing a baby. The infants are strapped to the mothers' seat belts via baby belts, and this makes them all cry. Once we are underway, dark-eyed toddlers run up and down the aisle. Four-year-old siblings herd the two-year-olds. It could be chaos, but everyone seems relaxed, so I guess it isn't.

Behind me two Russian businessmen ask the flight attendant for some alcohol. When they are told there is none available, they open up their duty-free whiskey. Before too long, they are pouring libations for the red-haired woman who sits next to me. The three of them get friendly, and then they offer the whiskey to me.

"No, thank you," I say. "I need to be a professional when I arrive." I will have dinner with the cultural attaché. I can't show up soused.

"We also will be professional," they say.

Across the aisle, the pretty young woman in traditional Tajik dress discreetly nurses her baby. Her four-year-old daughter is being pushed around in the aisle by another little girl in pigtails. I separate the two and send the victim back in the direction of her mother for protection. I am rewarded by a dazzling smile from the young woman.

"My husband has been studying in Moscow for two years," she says. "The children and I were there for a month, living in the dormitory."

"How do you like Moscow?"

"Home is better," she says.

"There are so many children on this plane," I say.

"Tajiks have big families, five or six children, maybe eight." She bounces her baby who has finished nursing. "I would like you to come visit me at my home."

Here is an invitation before I even land in Tajikistan. However, I can't accept, since this young woman lives outside of Dushanbe, and my five days in Tajikistan have been highly scheduled by the American Embassy.

"Well, make sure you see the Green Bazaar," she says.

We are flying over what remains of the Aral Sea, between Kazakhstan and Uzbekistan, a famous Soviet ecological disaster. Around the irregular coastline are large white patches.

"Is that snow?" I ask the red-haired Russian woman.

"No, salt. Everything that is white was previously water."

I search for the former island, now a peninsula, the Soviets used as a radioactive dump, but I can't distinguish it from the rest of this pale wasteland.

Later, we fly over mesmerizing snow-covered peaks for as far as I can see.

"My grandfather was sent to exile in Tajikistan," the Russian woman says. *"He saw that he had arrived in a beautiful place with a good climate. There were lots of fruits and vegetables. So, my family never left. Tajikistan is better than Russia."*

It's very hard to visualize Tajikistan as part of the Soviet Union. I had the misconception that the USSR was Slavic, or at least predominantly European; now I see how pan-national it was. Tajikistan looks, feels, and smells Central Asian rather than Soviet. The mountains surrounding Dushanbe are arid and rugged, similar to those of Afghanistan, not far away. On the streets of the capital, men loiter, squatting on the corners, just as they do everywhere in Asia. The women are striking in their traditional garb, long loose-fitting dresses in bright colors and sparkles. They wear matching trousers underneath, and many cover their heads with colorful scarves tied in the back. The women's dark hair frames their faces from under their scarves, and their arms and necks are often exposed. The men mostly wear western clothes, but some also cover their heads, according to Moslem tradition, with pillbox-shaped hats. This is definitely not Russia.

Yet, remnants of the Soviets are still evident. The capital was built from a small market town. *Dushanbe* means Monday, the market day. The Bolsheviks conquered the city in 1921; later the new city was called Stalinabad until Khrushchev debunked the Stalin cult and revived the city's market name. The political borders drawn up by the USSR divided the Tajik people, "to keep them weak," the attaché tells me. The main Tajik cities of Samarqand and Bukhara are now located in Uzbekistan, and Tajiks need a visa to visit them. *"Samarqand is ours,"* a taxi driver tells me. *"We don't like the Uzbeks."*

In the Soviet tradition, grand edifices line the main street, formerly called Lenin Street. *"This is the opera house, and here is the central library,"* Sharif, the Embassy driver, says, pointing to a prominent structure, *"with the busts of our great writers on the facade."*

"Who are the writers?" I ask.

He mentions several Persian poets and Gorky, a Soviet writer. A gargantuan monument dominates the square we are passing.

"Lenin is gone," he says with a chuckle. *"That monument is to Ismael Somoni."*

This country is a mixture. Islam may be resurgent, but I don't hear the call to prayer from the mosques, the way it resounds across the Moslem world. The Tajik language is written with Cyrillic script. Everyone also speaks Russian; their Tajik is peppered with enough Russian so that I can usually tell the subject of the conversation.

"Life was better under the USSR," several people tell me. *"There is no work here."* The attaché tells me that a large percentage of Tajik men are now working in Russia, where they fill the most menial jobs and are often discriminated against. I remember the derogatory comments of my Irkutsk colleagues about the immigrants working in the Chinese market. Tajik men go to Russia with the intention of sending money back to their families, but many disappear into the Russian underclass, take new wives, have families in Russia, and abandon their wives and children in Tajikistan.

As a guest of the embassy, I inhabit the strangely insulated world of the foreign service. An expeditor from the embassy meets me at customs. He hands me a welcome package from the embassy. It says that the threat of terror attacks is high. He hustles me through the process of obtaining a visa, and then passes me off to an armored vehicle and the driver Sharif. Even the US embassies don't buy American; the car is a four-wheel drive Toyota with a front-mounted antenna as thick as a baseball bat. The hatchback has a fortified inner door, and the windows don't open.

I am housed in a fancy hotel with a fake waterfall. There is a jacuzzi in my bathroom, and, wonder of all wonders, free internet access from a computer in my room. This room costs eighty dollars a night, an enormous fortune to Tajiks, many of whom earn as little as fifteen dollars a month.

The new American embassy is considered a prototype for US embassies in the Moslem world. For security reasons it is located on the outskirts of town rather than in the center near the other embassies. Cement blocks prevent anyone from driving too close. The first guard building contains Tajik employees in uniform. "Marines are not on the front line," the attaché says. This front building has riot gear, bulletproof vests and helmets, prominently hanging at the ready. I need to surrender my passport, my camera, and my flash drive in order to enter the embassy compound. All my possessions are put through an x-ray machine, and I must drink from my water bottle to prove that it is really water. Only then am I given a badge that says, "Escort required."

Before I can actually get to any office in the embassy, I need to pass through a courtyard, another waiting room manned by a Tajik, and then through an inner room where an invisible marine is on guard behind a dark bulletproof window. At each point, a secret code opens the next door. It isn't possible to get to the ladies room without a code and an escort.

One of my workshops with Tajik teachers is held in the embassy. During the first morning an alarm rings, repeatedly and urgently. The embassy employee in the room says it is a fire alarm. For a while I ignore it, assuming that someone from the Cultural Affairs office will come to escort us out of the building, but no one comes.

"We need to evacuate," says the embassy employee.

But the door to the corridor is locked. I can see the attaché through the glass door, but she indicates that she can't let us out. So ten Tajik English teachers and I are trapped in the corridor with the fire alarm screaming throughout the building.

Later, the head of security comes to explain the procedure. "When an alarm sounds," he says," all the doors immediately lock. It may be a false alarm, a trick to get everyone out of the building and ambush us. It may be a ruse to get everyone to evacuate in order to do some mischief in the embassy."

"So, what was the problem?" I ask.

"Some microwave popcorn."

For a Tajik, working at the embassy is probably one of the best paying jobs in Dushanbe.

"The overtime pay is good, too," Sharif says as he drives me to my next appointment. *"Then we get four dollars an hour."*

The Americans are on two-year tours of duty, but Gulya, whom I call my handler, has been working for the embassy for fifteen years. With her embassy salary, she gives financial support to her entire family: her husband, two children, son-in-law, grandson, father, several siblings, and nieces and nephews. "I am the most successful in the family," she says.

We are having lunch in an open-air marble teahouse. I have made the mistake of ordering lamb *shashlik*. It is dry and grizzly.

"Now that I have worked at the embassy for fifteen years," Gulya says, "I have earned the right to emigrate to the United States. My husband and my son, because he isn't yet twenty-one, can accompany me. My son is crazy to go, but I feel great conflict. I will cry if I leave this country."

The long term Tajik employees like Gulya are probably the people who actually keep the embassy running. Gulya seems to understand her own importance. She moves through Tajik society with tremendous assurance. When we go to the Green Bazaar, she tastes handfuls of everything: pecans, walnuts, almonds, dates, prunes, figs, all different types of raisins in great heaps, dried and fresh mulberries, tiny green apricots. She calls on the merchants to explain to me the difference between Tajik and Iranian pistachios. She pinches all the different types of bread. They are baked in clay ovens and are round and flat with different patterns perforated into them. All the vendors are eager for me to taste as well, but I feel ashamed to sample their wares and not to buy.

Gulya shrugs. "This is the bazaar," she says.

I put a salted roasted apricot pit in my mouth. "*Nyet!*" the merchant and Gulya cry simultaneously before I can bite into it. "You must crack it open first."

The tiny native pistachios are quite delicious, almost like pine nuts, so I ask for a hundred grams, but the merchant insists that it is a gift.

"*Your president Bush is making a lot of trouble,*" one fruit merchant tells me in Russian.

I agree.

"*He is killing innocent people.*"

"*Soon there will be an election and things will change,*" I feel like I should cross my fingers behind my back. "*My president is very unpopular with the American people.*"

All the nearby merchants are listening to me. Gulya represents the US embassy.

"*I hope we elect someone who will end the war,*" I say. "*Inshallah.*" God willing.

This seems to satisfy him.

The plane to Khujand is scheduled to fly at 6:30 PM after I have given an all-day workshop in Dushanbe. I am supposed to give another long workshop the next day. But by the time we get to the airport, it is raining, and so the plane will not take off. The airport officials lock the doors to the waiting room with a large padlock and leave the building, abandoning us all to sit on windowsills for hours. Finally Gulya gives her phone number to another passenger, a stranger. "We'll go out for dinner," she tells me. "He will call me if they start loading."

About 11 PM, the man calls to say that a decision will be made soon. We rush back to the airport, but the plane has been postponed until the following morning. Some people will spend the night at the airport. Maybe they will be allowed into a waiting room. The driver takes me back to the hotel.

At 4 AM the phone rings. "I just heard from the passenger," Gulya says. "They are starting to load the plane."

Although I complained bitterly about the delay the previous night, I now see why they didn't fly in the rain. Our flight is in a two-engine prop plane that seems to be made of cardboard. It flies low over the magnificent snow-capped peaks, rattling and roaring, but the flight is smooth, and we arrive without incident. The Khujand airport is located in the outskirts of the city where there is a closed Soviet uranium plant.

"But what about the radiation?" I ask, trying not to breathe.

Gulya nods her head. "Some people got sick. But now people want to live in these houses because they are nice and the rent is low."

Our driver is a very young man who has a small DVD monitor installed on his dashboard. He drives with one eye on the road and one on the action movie on his screen. There are no seatbelts.

Gulya is from the Khujand area and will not be returning with me to Dushanbe. After my workshop, she is very proud to bring me to the ancient mosque and the enormous pink bazaar with tiled mosaics. She buys several different types of bread for her father and sister. Later we take our bread to an outdoor café and eat it with soup.

Back at the Khujand airport, she hustles me to the front of all the lines, proclaiming that I am an important guest of the US embassy. No one protests. In Tajikistan, ladies are always allowed to board first anyway. When I am in my seat ready for take off, a distinguished-looking gray-haired man slips into the seat next to me.

"You are Vivian?" he says in English. "I am Gulya's colleague from the US embassy. I just met her, and she told me to take care of you."

I really don't want any help. Sharif will meet the plane in Dushanbe. I look out the window at the mountains.

"I have also worked at the embassy for fifteen years," he says, "in the political sector."

I suppose I'm tired and grouchy from only four hours of sleep.

"I am sixty years old," he says, "but I feel young. I have four daughters and two grandsons. I want to get a new wife of thirty-five, so she will give me a son. My wife will have to share. Sometimes she says she is willing, but sometimes she isn't."

"Maybe you should be satisfied with your grandsons."

When the plane lands, I try to give him the slip. "Vivian," he calls, "wait for me. I will go in the embassy car with you."

My last day in Tajikistan, I take a taxi outside of Dushanbe, past rolling hills of vineyards to the Gissar Fort, a red clay-and-brick ruin supposedly 2,500 years old. This was the ancient center of the market town of Dushanbe. Next to the fort are remnants of a madrasa, a mosque, and the ruins of a hostel for the merchants who traveled the Silk Road. The Bolsheviks blew up the fort when a nationalist leader took refuge there in his fight against Russian takeover. Behind its gateway, turrets, and ramparts lies a bowl-shaped field. The remnants of the walls of the fort circle this basin where cows and goats graze and a young woman collects dung for fuel. From the ramparts I look out at the snow-peaked mountains circling the Dushanbe valley. I am in a far off place, in a land full of contradictions. History has had its way with Tajikistan. It's terribly impoverished, but the land is fertile, and the people have a graceful calm about them. I've given four days of workshops with English teachers, had a meeting with the Ambassador, an online chat with teachers and students, a visit with students at the American Corner. The teachers work under difficult conditions with no materials, a curriculum dictated by politicians, a heavy workload, low salaries. Yet teachers and students have listened to me eagerly and have been enthusiastic participants in all the activities. They especially loved analyzing "Stopping By Woods on a Snowy Evening," which I presented as an example of using poetry to teach pronunciation. From New England to Tajikistan.

"Priyezhiti yesho," everyone says to me. *"Come back again."*

When I open my email in Moscow, there is a message from the cultural attaché. "Thank you so much for your expertise, energy, and flexibility," she says. "Let me know anytime you are interested in returning."

Angarsk plane, Siberia. 2008

On the train in Ukraine,
en route to Moscow
May 2, 2008

A Look into the Past

Since my flight from Dushanbe brings me back to Moscow, I have the opportunity to take a week's vacation and visit my friends in Ukraine. It is 6:30 on Saturday morning; three Ukrainians who should be asleep after a long work week are standing on the train platform waiting for me. By the time I make my way down the corridor to the exit of the car, they have located *platzkart,* third class wagon number five. Four steep steps and I am in their arms. They are Svetlana, Natasha, and thirteen-year-old Dasha, who carries a bouquet of red tulips. They whisk me into a waiting taxi. In a few minutes I am in an attractive apartment Svetlana has reserved for me in the university dormitory. She has stocked the kitchen with salami, bread, tea, and sparkling water. Natasha adds bananas and a local SIM card to convert my Russian cell phone. I am back home in Poltava, Ukraine.

I have traveled from the US to Irkutsk to Moscow three times and to Tajikistan before I have managed to arrive in Poltava, but it has always been in my mind to return to this place. My time is short; the schedule of social events is tight. Some days I must triple book in an attempt to see everyone. By Friday noon I'll be back on the train for the eighteen hour return trip to Moscow. A whirlwind stay, but a warm breeze of friendship after months of Siberia.

Natasha and I crisscross the city on foot, so I can absorb everything, the familiar and the new, since my last stay three years ago. Poltava is blooming with tulips. At the white monument at

161

the end of October Street, the lilacs are just about to burst open as are the white cone-shaped flowers of the chestnut trees. The park in the center has been planted and mowed, groomed for the Orthodox Easter. The central market is abuzz with pre-holiday shopping. Easter *paska* breads, cylindrical with white icing and colored sprinkles, are everywhere.

There are signs of prosperity in Poltava. The underground mall, half empty three years ago, now seems filled with stores. There are many new apartment buildings with elegant penthouses and attractive glass balconies. A huge coral-colored building now dwarfs the university, making it look dowdy and old-fashioned with its Khrushchev cement block architecture.

The Grand Supermarket, a fledgling business on my first trip in 2001, has moved down the street to larger quarters. It now sells peanut butter from Poland. I haven't seen peanut butter since January, so I quickly grab a jar. When I tell Natasha of my discovery, she picks up a jar as well. I return to buy a second jar to take to Siberia, and Natasha's friend takes one too. The guard looks at me suspiciously, not understanding the run on peanut butter. There's one jar left; maybe he will try it himself.

Since the breakup of the Soviet Union, stores have opened and closed in Poltava in rapid succession, but now there seems to be more stability. The camera shop up the stairs on October Street is still open. The grocery near the university still offers its succulent rotisseried chickens. The craft store with its clay Ukrainian caricatures and enameled eggs still invites browsers. There are two new cafes offering gourmet coffee, and down the street from the university is an internet café called Maximum.

At the central market my friend Varvara looks as glamorous as ever; she measures dried fruit and nuts into plastic bags with long blue artificial fingernails. I'm not sure I will recognize my cheese lady without her purple winter hat, but as I head for the cheese section, there she is, with her beautiful bleached hair and her thick blue eye shadow. She smiles as if I had been there last week.

It is a week of excessive Ukrainian hospitality from both old friends and total strangers. *Pirozhi* and *verenikis*, homemade pickles, salads, sausages, cognac, vodka. The Easter *paska* bread is passed around like currency. The line outside the bakery goes up the stairs and into the street. Nothing is being sold except *paska*. Buying it seems infectious. They come in all sizes, as small as a cupcake, as big as a basketball. I enter the bakery to purchase one to bring to Easter dinner at Svetlana's, but when my turn on the line arrives, I take three, a little fat one and two long tall ones. Of course, Svetlana already has three at her house. Then another guest Tanya presents me with a yellow iced *paska*. It has a plastic cross on top.

"*I baked this and it was blessed at the church,*" she says.

My first Russian teacher, Lyubov, a renowned baker, arrives at my apartment with a big round one loaded with sprinkles.

"*I made this for you,*" she says.

When Natasha returns from her mother's country home, she brings me another homemade *paska*, a gift from her mother along with fresh eggs and sorrel from the garden.

"What do people do with all these *paski?*" I ask an English teacher, Anna.

"They have been blessed. We must eat them."

"But I have three."

"We cut them up and dry them. Then we eat them with tea. They stay good for a long time."

I must look doubtful because Anna adds, "Or you can donate them to someone who has no food."

When I return to the dorm, I arrange a still life of all the gifts: three *paski*, four ceramic elephants, a Ukrainian lady salt dispenser, two boxes of chocolate, all standing on a calendar of drawings of Gogol's buxom heroines.

On Tuesday I have an invitation from Viktoriya, an English teacher from the foreign language faculty at the university.

"Since I saw you last," she says, "I have gotten divorced."

"I'm sorry to hear that."

"Well, now I have a new man friend, and he will take us to the aerodrome."

Ivan is a distinguished-looking man who stands very erect. Viktoriya tells me he was a captain in the Soviet army. The two of them have practiced his presentation about the military history of the aerodrome; Viktoriya is planning to translate.

"No translating," I say in Russian. *"If I don't understand, I'll ask you."*

At first Viktoriya cannot believe that I really intend to speak Russian with Ivan, but by the end of the day, she is speaking with me in Russian herself.

The aerodrome was off limits to civilians until the breakup of the Soviet Union, and it is still guarded by Ukrainian military. At the entrance Ivan gets out of the car and negotiates something with the guard to allow the gate to be opened. Ivan tells me that American soldiers were quartered in this area during World War II. There was a joint war effort between Soviet and American soldiers. *"Americans were bombing Koenigsberg, and Soviets were bombing Berlin,"* he says. *"We were working together."*

The driver turns onto an old runway. I am in the front passenger seat for the best view, although, knowing how Ukrainians drive, I would prefer a back seat.

164

A heavy rain is falling. The runway is quite slick. Like a child playing with a toy car, the driver revs his engine. He picks up speed and barrels down the runway, as if he might take flight.

Abruptly he careens off the runway and squeals to a stop in front of a small fleet of fighter planes. There are some plaques and what look like ordinance lying on the ground. It seems to be a military museum.

"The people cried when America destroyed the planes after the breakup of the Soviet Union," Ivan says.

"But why did they cry?" I had thought Ukraine wanted to get rid of their stockpiled weapons.

Under an umbrella Ivan walks me to a slender pointy-nosed plane. To my untrained eye it seems to be a prop plane.

"There is no other country in the world that has a plane like this," Ivan says. *"That's why America is so afraid."*

"Is this a modern plane?"

"Modern, completely modern. It is the best in the world, and America doesn't have anything like this." He watches for my reaction. *"America is very afraid,"* he repeats.

"But," I say, *"I don't think America is very afraid of Ukraine."*

"Oh, yes. Very afraid," he says in a gruff tone.

President Bush has recently been to Ukraine. In Russia, there was great outrage about his suggestion that Ukraine join NATO.

"I think America fears Iran more than Ukraine," I say.

Now I have insulted him. He barks to the caretaker who produces a page of statistics. *"This plane is capable of flying ten thousand kilometers and can stay in the air for twelve hours,"* Yuri says.

"Ten thousand kilometers," Ivan repeats when I don't respond. *"It's easy to bomb Alaska."*

"But Ukraine isn't near Alaska."

"From Sakhalin."

"But Sakhalin is not in Ukraine." It's a Russian island in the Pacific, probably eight thousand kilometers or more from Poltava.

"We are Slavs," Ivan says puffing up his chest and crossing his arms. *"I am Orthodox. And no one will ever ever make me change to become Catholic."*

Later Viktoriya apologizes. "We rehearsed what he would say, and I looked up all the technical words so I could translate. But Ivan deviated from the script," she says.

After the tour Viktoriya takes me to dinner at the home of two of her students Sasha and Olga. The mother, Lydia, tells me what a great honor it is to have an American stranger in her home. In Ukrainian style we are seated on couches in the living room in front of a table nearly collapsing with salads, smoked and fresh fish, roast chicken, dumplings. The mother and grandmother have been cooking all day. They also have a Norwegian man, Knut, staying with them. Every few minutes Lydia says in English, "I want let's drink," and she flicks her neck with her thumb and forefinger.

Eighteen-year-old Sasha is the man of the house, so for the third toast, traditionally the toast to the ladies, he stands up and insists that Knut get to his feet. "To the most beautiful women in the world," Sasha says gamely in English. Around the table sit his mother, his sister, his old grandmother, his teacher, and a sixty-year-old American woman he has never seen before. The Norwegian man would rather say how happy he is to be a guest in the home, but Sasha reminds him he must toast to the women.

We are having a jolly time in English and Russian, and then the talk turns to politics. Sasha has seen a movie that claims that the events of September 11 never really happened.

Knut is outraged. "I have absolutely no doubt that the events occurred," he says.

"Only three people died," Sasha says. "It has been proven that planes couldn't bring down such strong buildings."

Lydia works in a construction industry job, so she is an expert even if she is the bookkeeper. "*It isn't possible,*" she agrees.

"The buildings were bombed from within," Olga says.

"Everyone in Ukraine has seen this movie," Viktoriya says.

"I'm just stating the facts," Sasha says.

"I was in New York on September 21," I say. "The city was plastered with posters begging for information about all the people who were missing. I know a young boy who was at Stuyvesant High School and watched the planes hit the buildings. Why don't you consider the evidence from the survivors who evacuated the buildings? Some of the people below the point of impact escaped."

"There were survivors?" Sasha says.

"I want let's drink," says Lydia.

It's strange to me how people determine that facts are indisputable. At Easter dinner everyone said that life was better under the Soviets.

"*We all lived together happily as one big nation,*" Tanya said.

"But now they are just doing nothing in Kiev," Svetlana said. "In Belarus it is much better."

My understanding is that the leader of Belarus is a Stalin-type dictator. "What about the slave labor camps under the Soviets?" I asked Svetlana. I had just finished reading Solzhenitsyn.

"I don't know, so I can't say if it is true."

Now at Lydia's dinner, her son says, "*Stalin wasn't responsible for the terrors. It was Beria. Stalin just signed his name.*" I heard Irina Fyodorovna in Irkutsk express this same mythology.

167

Conversations like these remind me that Ukraine has not traveled so far from its Soviet past. On the other hand, Ukraine is actually experiencing its own messy form of democracy. That the government doesn't speak with one voice, the very thing Svetlana deprecates, is an indication of the fledgling democracy in Ukraine. In Russia there is no sign of this cacophony and virtually no sign of democracy.

In Ukraine, however, Natasha is free to speak up. "During the time of the Orange Revolution," she says as we pass the statue of Lenin on one last walk, "for the first time in my life I felt that I could make a difference. I was so proud to vote. Some people have forgotten what it was like under the Soviet Union. They deny that Stalin created the famine that killed so many people in Ukraine. But he absolutely created it."

On Friday I am back on the train. As a woman traveling alone, I choose to travel in a third class sleeping car. The *platzkarts* are open cars filled with double-decker berths, four beds for each doorless section, and two more against the windows across the aisle. Instead of a maximum of 18 passengers in a car in first class, there are three times that many in *platzkart*. However, there are no closed doors, so societal pressure discourages harassment. I find my berth and settle in for the long trip overnight to Moscow and then overnight again by plane to Irkutsk, two consecutive nights in transit. In my suitcase is a beautiful damask tablecloth, a gift from Natasha, for our Thanksgiving table in Massachusetts.

There have been more invitations in one week in Ukraine than in four months in Irkutsk, more invitations than I could accept. I skated at a new rink with Dasha and Natasha on the last ice of the season. I visited Varvara and her sons who were worried a high-rise apartment building would displace them from their private home. Varvara showed me the latest letters she had received in her eternal hunt for an internet husband. Natasha and I paid our respects to the bust of Pushkin in Birch Square. We walked the three kilometers to the monastery and discovered that there was a magnificent collection of icons in the basement of one of the churches. Some of the life-sized icons were headless because the Soviets had decapitated them and used their wooden bodies for floorboards. Natasha, young Dasha, and I ate *kachapuria* and *shashlick* at our favorite Georgian restaurant where we asked the waiter to take the same photograph of us as three years ago. My old teacher Lyubov drank tea in my apartment and gratified me by marveling at my progress in Russian. Svetlana's son drove me to their *dacha*, where I could see the cherry trees in bloom and the potato plants sprouting. There I admired the plum tree I had helped plant eight years ago. They call it "Vivian's tree." This year there are blossoms on it for the first time.

The sleeping car is filling up. A vigorous-looking man with a potbelly will sleep above me. A man in a black leather jacket takes the other top berth. Across the corridor a couple sit two on one seat, and across the table from them sits a dark serious-faced man. A young pregnant woman and her two-year-old son come through, counting places until she deposits herself and her little boy in the berth immediately opposite my own. There are introductions all around. The young woman's husband, who is staying behind, makes several trips to the compartment, bringing a crib, a stroller, a tricycle, stuffing them onto the third level above our heads. The final item is the potty; the young mother places it at the ready on the floor in the space between us. The husband leaves, and the train lurches forward.

Four soldiers, Saint Petersburg, Russia. 2008

Victory Day for the Great Patriotic War

May ninth is Victory Day for the Great Patriotic War in Defense of the Fatherland. It is known as V-E Day in the US, marking the end of World War II in Europe.

"It's the biggest holiday of the year," Anton, the English teacher, says.

"A lot of drunken people walking in the streets," my friend Alex says. In Russian class we learn a ditty to practice our pronunciation.
To the parade, delighted
Goes the drummer,
Full of happiness.
He drums! He drums!
Ninety minutes without stopping.

Banners bedeck Kirov Square, the center of Irkutsk. Vendors sell flowers, balloons, toys. *Kvas,* the fermented drink made of stale bread, is sold from round tanks that look like small oil trucks. *"Congratulations to the Veterans!"* The signs are all over the city. For the first time, I see the red flags with the hammer and sickle. It's not possible to celebrate this holiday without applauding the Soviet Union for its victory over the Fascists.

A huge crowd waits opposite the Soviet-style administration building, where a review stand has been erected. People climb onto fences, railings, and roofs. They hang out the windows of all the official buildings. Canned patriotic music blares from a loudspeaker. As I squeeze myself into the crowd, I see troops at attention, facing the reviewing stand, their backs to us.

Old men, in dress uniforms with all their decorations, sit in a row next to the stand. These veterans are in their eighties or nineties by now. Some are in wheelchairs. Many are being attended by wives or daughters.

Finally the officials and commanding officers mount the reviewing stand, and the canned music is replaced by the live music of a military band. *Barabanit! Barabanit!* He drums! He drums! Two jeeps circle the parade ground, each with an officer standing in the back in a salute. The soldiers return the salute as the officers pass. Then the troops march around the square in succession. I remember watching news clips of the enormous Soviet military parades in Moscow during the Cold War. This is Irkutsk's twenty-first century version. One plane flies over the parade. Its landing gear is down. Everyone takes photos, but to me it looks like a passenger plane about to land at the airport.

Behind me a young boy on his father's shoulders gives a commentary of the parade. This is helpful because I can barely see.

"Soldiers in blue. Now the green ones," the boy says. *"Now another blue group. Now black. The women."*

"Where are the women?" his father asks, craning his neck. *"Oh, those aren't women. They're girls."*

The soldiers all look extremely young, pink-faced, the boys' hair cropped close. We are crammed on the spot where the cathedral was destroyed by the Communists in 1932. The Soviet Union fought a long war in Afghanistan; post-Soviet Russia has also had a war in Chechnya, but The War always means World War II to the Russians. Young men with limbs missing, the veterans of Chechnya, are begging at the central market. They are not included in this tribute to the military. Only the veterans of the Great Patriotic War receive flowers and seats of honor.

The old wartime songs tell of the lonely terrifying life at the Front. Did the people of this city feel far removed from the war, the way many Americans feel about the war in Iraq, or did it dominate their consciousness? Their fathers, sons, brothers and husbands were transported more than three thousand miles from Irkutsk. Almost half didn't return. On the WWII memorial plaque behind the administration building, it says, *"There was no front here, only grief and black days."* The history of the Soviet Front is both heroic and horrific: twenty million soldiers lost, desperate gulag prisoners given the option of escape from labor camps if they would serve, orders for soldiers to shoot their own retreating troops, returned prisoners-of-war treated as spies and sent to slave labor camps. Irkutsk's prison transfer station saw a steady stream of prisoners, many of them recent war heroes, on their way to the gulag.

Elena tells me the story of her father, who in the first days of the war was sent to the border. Hitler's attack on Russia had ambushed Stalin after the signing of the German-Russian non-aggression treaty, but it was seditious to doubt the strategy of the Supreme Leader. To a fellow soldier, Elena's father expressed dismay at the small number of Russian troops providing them support. The comrade reported Elena's father's words of doubt; he was arrested as a spy. Initially he was to be shot, but his sentence was commuted to ten years hard labor. Even after he served his term, he was still forbidden from returning to his home in Leningrad.

"I was born in exile," Elena says. *"Everyone in my class was either the child of an ex-prisoner or of a prison guard. No one can tell me the gulags didn't exist."*

On the other hand, the Soviets bore the full brunt of the war against Hitler. The memorial at the eternal flame has flat stones, like grave markers, for all the Siberians who died in far off places, one for all the men buried in Yugoslavia, one for the Albanian graves, for the Italian graves, seventeen countries in all.

At the parade the announcer calls out each regiment and where it fought. The unit that fought the Great Patriotic War in Defense of the Fatherland in Volgograd. The unit that fought the Great Patriotic War in Defense of the Fatherland in Sevastopol, in Kiev, in Minsk, in Odessa, and on and on. The young troops step up and march around the square. These are men who were babies at the time of the breakup of the USSR. Whom are they training to fight now?

There is no easy reaction to this celebration; it is too fraught with contradictions. The crowd is hushed, watching the young marchers. My ninety-year-old father-in-law was an infantryman in what the Russians call the Second Front, the invasion of Normandy. Hank slogged his way ashore on Omaha Beach on D-Day Plus Four, the fifth day of the invasion. The American troops who landed on D-Day itself were basically cannon fodder, sacrificed to allow the future waves of the invasion to solidify a beachhead from which to fight. Hank has his silver star he keeps in a box in a drawer. He had to hunt for it one day when the grandchildren wanted to see it. It was awarded to him for bravery in neutralizing a German machine gun nest that was preventing the invading American troops from advancing up the beach. Hank, the gentlest of men, will never talk about his experiences during the war. We know he marched across Europe or rode on the backs of tanks and trucks in combat much of the way. Hank could be one of the old men sitting across from us now, but he has never wanted to attend a Veterans Day or Memorial Day parade.

The troops exit the square to our left, disappearing behind the administration building en route to the war memorial with its eternal flame. Last to leave is the band corps, playing as they march. The cymbalist wears spike heels. The saxophonist wears a miniskirt. They step to the drumbeat. *Barabanchik ochen rad. Barabanit, barabanit!*

The canned music takes over again. "It's the final countdown!" Hard rock in English blares from the speakers. "The final countdown!" Two army trucks thunder around the parade ground; martial arts experts in camouflage uniforms emerge for a choreographed display. They pretend to bring each other down with athletic leaps and kicks. They shoot and stab each other with bayonets. They roll and parry and kick and punch. They jump through burning hoops and neutralize machine gun nests.

Finally the crowd disperses. I try to get closer to the old veterans, and I am not alone in this. Television announcers lower their booms for interviews. Strangers from the crowd present the veterans with roses and carnations. At the monument, children place flowers on the plaques: those lost in Romania, those lost in Hungary, those lost in Czechoslovakia, those lost in Bulgaria.

Two elegant elderly women in spring hats accompany a distinguished-looking veteran. I can't tell his rank from his uniform, but his chest is covered with medals. These three have the bearing of patricians. The woman who seems to be his wife wears a green hat with a wide brim and high-heeled boots. Her scarf and gloves are starkly white. Her bouquet of red carnations is brilliant against her dark coat. Two girls approach and offer these three more flowers. As if they are movie stars, the girls ask if they can pose with this veteran and his relatives for a photograph. The elderly trio graciously agrees. From a distance I snap a picture of them as well.

The woman in the green hat smiles at me, nodding that I am welcome to take their picture. Then she brings her husband to me. "*Let's take a picture together,*" she says. She and her husband pose with me as passersby take photos. "*Where are you from?*" she asks me.

"*From America.*"

"*This picture will go to America,*" the officer says with a laugh.

"*Thank you for posing with us,*" the woman in the green hat says.

One of my students from English class approaches me. "Can I have my picture taken with you?" Begzat asks.

Next comes Maya, another English student. "May I have a photo with you?"

Then comes Han Yan from my Russian class.

The foreign English teacher or a Great Patriotic War veteran. It's a fleeting opportunity to get a historic photograph.

Dock woman, Russky Island, Russian Far East. 2008

Farewell to Irkutsk

At the Office for International Relations, I tell them I will
depart on Monday, June twenty-third.

"For good?" the blond woman named Zena asks.

"For good."

International Relations has always insisted on holding my visa
in their files. It has made me feel I cannot go anywhere without
their permission. That is probably the way they want me to feel.

"Did you buy your ticket?" Zena says. *"I need to see it."*

I guess she doesn't believe me. Maybe she is afraid I will try to
stay in Russia as an illegal immigrant.

"And I need proof that you returned all your library books."

"But I never had permission to take out any library books."

*"The kommandant of the dorm needs to verify that you leave all
the silverware."*

"But there wasn't any silverware. I had to buy it myself."

I am gratified to see that when I am angry my Russian is better now than it was at the beginning of the semester. Neverthe-
less, I have no choice but to run in circles getting all the signatures
and stamps she requires.

For six months I have been the only constant inhabitant in
this apartment on the fourth floor of dorm number four. Several Russians, a German, a Belgian, and an Italian have used the
other bedrooms at different times, but no one has stayed more
than a couple of weeks. It has always been my apartment with my
clothesline draped across the washroom, my dish drainer in the
kitchen sink, and my shoes and coat in the hall. The plastic screws

on my spongy blue toilet seat are starting to strip, but they only have to last a few more days.

I have rattled around the four bedrooms, sleeping in three different ones over the course of the semester. Room 414, my first assigned spot, was freezing at -30°C/-22°F in January. As soon as I got the opportunity, I moved to 412. But then the electric power station, the *transformator*, on the street kept me awake with its noxious hum and, even more, with the thought of its magnetic field somehow rearranging the atoms in my body.

So I moved to 415, my current room. It overlooks the quad of dilapidated dormitories. From this room I can't hear the electrical hum. When the snow melted, a body of a dead cat appeared on the ground outside my window. Perhaps it died of the cold and got buried by the snow. I saw the corpse every day, and then one day it was gone.

Now Frank has returned. The birch trees outside the window have sprung into leaf; the pear tree is flowering. Below, as the evenings get longer and warmer, the students gather to laugh and talk and kiss. Each morning, beer bottles are strewn all over the grass. Eventually they break, and broken glass is everywhere.

"Frank showed us a photo of the place you are living," my friend Gail writes from Massachusetts. "It's so depressing."

But, I haven't been depressed here. This is just life in Russia.

Frank and I take Alex to dinner at a Chinese restaurant. As a farewell gift, he brings me a copy of his catalog of Siberian plants with his own illustrations in line drawings. I present him with a book to prepare for the TOEFL test so he can improve his English and someday apply for a Fulbright grant to study in the US. Alex orders the food, so we eat greasy lamb and a salad of cockscomb and cucumbers. We drink a liter of vodka, chased with pineapple juice.

Alex toasts to my return to Irkutsk. He has to shout over the singer, a young man with a velvet, highly amplified, voice.

"I think you will be back," Alex says.

Frank toasts Alex for taking care of me here in Irkutsk.

"That was easy," Alex says.

I toast Alex's arrival in the US someday on his own Fulbright grant.

"My favorite toast," he says.

The vodka goes down surprisingly smoothly. It loosens Alex's tongue, and he tells me about his fifty-four-year-old girlfriend, Natasha, a simultaneous translator of English. She is supposed to help him with his preparation for the TOEFL test. Natasha doesn't like Alex's friends, and she has refused to meet me.

"I haven't seen her in a month," he says. *"We broke up."*

A cute Buriyat woman with an exposed round belly and high heels jiggles her way up to the empty dance floor. With graceful, loose limbs, her partner swings her.

Alex wants me to dance. *"You need to try everything,"* he says.

I've heard that before. But I won't dance with Alex in a Russian club after drinking too much vodka. So he dances by himself. Later he walks us back to the dorm. We decide he will write to me in Russian, and I will write in English.

"I'm very glad," he says as I kiss him on the cheek and give him a hug.

At the university the teachers are frantic because the US embassy has asked them to host an English Language Summer Institute. Irina Fyodorovna asks me to give two presentations on Monday afternoon, the day I am leaving, and she wants Frank to act as university photographer for the day. Three days later, I will give another presentation at the conference in Vladivostok, almost two thousand miles to the east. Then it's west to Moscow and home.

"We want and need Vivian to come back," Irina Fyodorovna says to the group, "but she won't promise." Everyone looks at me.

"I don't know yet," I say. "It's very far."

Cinema cafe, Vladivostok, Russian Far East. 2008

Epilogue

Back in Ashfield, the walks across the icy field remind me of the silent nights in the village on Lake Baikal. The New England sky is cold and clear, the forest still. In Irkutsk the women must be walking down the streets in their long fur coats.

An email arrives from a German teacher who worked briefly at the university in Irkutsk and stayed in my apartment in the dormitory. He has been back to Irkutsk for another short stint. "I stayed in your apartment again," he writes. "But your toilet seat is no longer there. And even more disturbing, I went to the American Studies office to give them your regards, but there was no one there who remembered you."

The snow crunches beneath my feet.

Glossary

Amerikanskye gora
    rollercoaster (literally-American mountains)

Babushka (plural *babushki*)
    grandmother

Banya
    Russian style sauna

Blini
    thin pancakes, often stuffed with farmer cheese

Borscht
    Russian or Ukrainian beet and cabbage soup

Buterbrodi
    open-faced sandwiches

Chai
    tea

Dacha
    summer cottage

Dezhurnaya
    woman on duty in the dormitory

Dofu
    tofu

Elektrichka
    electric railway

Greven (plural *grevna*)
    Ukrainian currency

Inshallah
    God willing (Arabic)

Kachapuria
    Georgian bread

Katanye
    sledding hill

Kefir
> drink made of fermented milk

Kimchi
> Korean pickle

Kommandant
> head housekeeper in the dormitory

Kvas
> drink made of fermented bread

Lavosh
> flat bread

Luego
> later (Spanish)

Marshrutka (plural *marshrutki*)
> mini-bus

Nerpa
> fresh water seal unique to Lake Baikal

Nye rabotaet.
> It doesn't work.

Omul
> fish unique to Lake Baikal

Paska (plural *paski*)
> Easter bread

Patom
> later

Pho
> Vietnamese soup

Pilmeni
> Russian ravioli

Pirozhi
> small pies filled with meat, potato, or cabbage

Platzkart
> third class sleeping cars on the trains

Plov
> pilaf, rice cooked with vegetables

Po-russkie
> in Russian (literally-in the Russian way)

Priyatnovo appetita.
> Have a good meal. (*Bon appétit.*)

Priyezhiti yesho.
> Come again.

Provodnika
> train conductor

Pyatnitza
> Friday

Sala
> lard

Shashlik
> shish kebab

Subbota
> Saturday

Taiga
> Siberian forest

Tarzanka
> rope swing or slide

Ti
> you (familiar)

Tiepló
> warm (temperature)

Transformator
> power station

Universityet
university
Vagon
train car
Vereniki
Ukrainian ravioli
Vi
you (polite or plural)
Vi ashiblis nomerom.
You have the wrong number.
Visky
whiskey
Voskryeshenye
Sunday

Acknowledgments

This book would not have been possible without the support and generosity of many. Tobey Ward served as a gentle but merciless editor.

Roland Merullo gave me my first lesson in Russian and inspired me to persevere with my Russian studies and my writing. The professors of the Russian departments of Mount Holyoke College, Amherst College, and Smith College—Edwina Cruise, Peter Scotto, Susan Downing, Ekaterina Dianina, Stanley Rabinowitz, Tatyana Babyonyshev, Viktoria Schweitzer, and Catherine Woronzoff-Dashkoff—have shown great generosity in allowing me to participate in their classes.

I want to thank Olena Bashmakova, Valentyna Semyrog, Olga Kovalchuk, Nadezhda Ovsyanyk, and Sergey Kalyuzhny for their friendship and support with my endless study of Russian. Kathleen Holmes read the essays and first connected me with Marcia Gagliardi and Mary-Ann DeVita Palmieri of Haley's. Varvara Chernuka is an inspiration for her work, limitless hospitality, and her friendship. Candida Johnson made my first trip to Ukraine possible and shared her beloved Poltava with me.

I have utmost gratitude and appreciation for the teachers of Russian at the International Faculty and the teachers in the Department of American Studies of Irkutsk State Linguistic University and for the teachers in the Foreign Language Chair at Poltava University of Consumer Cooperatives in the Ukraine.

This book would not have been possible without the support of the excellent Fulbright Scholar Program, the Fulbright offices in Washington and Moscow, and the administration of Holyoke Community College.

Most of all, I am grateful to my husband Frank Ward and our two children Tobey and Caleb for their loving encouragement and patience, even during my absences.

Vivian Leskes

About the Author

Vivian Leskes is Professor of English as a Second Language at Holyoke Community College in Massachusetts. She lived and worked in Siberia in 2008 on a Fulbright grant. Currently, she and her husband, photographer Frank Ward, live in Western Massachusetts.

The author at -30°F.

Text for *Lost in Siberia,* set inAdobe Jenson Pro, captures the
essence of Nicolas Jenson's roman and
Ludovico degli Arrighi's italic typeface designs.
The combined strength and beauty of these two icons of
Renaissance type result in an elegant typeface suited to a
broad spectrum of applications. Designed by
Robert Slimbach of the Adobe type design team,
Adobe Jenson Pro is part of the family of Adobe Originals
historical revivals, including Adobe Garamond Pro and
Adobe Caslon Pro. With its many OpenType features,
extended language support, and typographic refinement,
Adobe Jenson Pro provides a power and flexibility for
text composition rarely found in digital type.
Titles are set in ITC Kabel. Designed by Rudolf Koch and
released in 1927 by the Klingspor foundry in Germany,
Kabel is named in honor of the laying of the first
trans-Atlantic telephone cable.
In 1975, under special license from D. Stempel AG, the
International Typeface Corporation redrew the family and
added a fifth weight. Geometric proportions are combined
with humanistic features in this
unusual sans serif typeface.
ITC Kabel has a very large x-height.

Breinigsville, PA USA
17 January 2011
253468BV00002B/1/P